THE SCRUM HALF OF MY LIFE

The Scrum Half of My Life

An Autobiography

Steve Smith
with
Geoff Green

Stanley Paul
London Melbourne Sydney Auckland Johannesburg

To my most loyal and most biased fans – my mother, father and sister
Susan.

Stanley Paul & Co. Ltd
An imprint of the Hutchinson Publishing Group
17–21 Conway Street, London W1P 6JD

Hutchinson Publishing Group (Australia) Pty Ltd
PO Box 496, 16–22 Church Street, Hawthorne, Melbourne,
Victoria 3122
PO Box 151, Broadway, New South Wales 2007

Hutchinson Group (NZ) Ltd
32–34 View Road, PO Box 40–086, Glenfield, Auckland 10

Hutchinson Group (SA) Pty Ltd
PO Box 337, Bergvlei 2012, South Africa

First published 1984
© Steve Smith 1984

Set in Baskerville by Tradespools Ltd, Frome, Somerset

Printed and bound in Great Britain by Anchor Brendon Ltd,
Tiptree, Essex

ISBN 0 09 159220 8

Contents

Acknowledgements

I would like to thank Geoff Green, Rugby Union correspondent of the *Manchester Evening News*, for his invaluable assistance in writing this autobiography. We have known each other since I was a teenager and both enjoyed looking back over my playing career, interspersed as it has been by several historic and totally unforgettable rugby occasions. Fortified by an endless stream of coffee supplied by his wife, Barbara, I bared my soul on tape and Geoff faithfully committed my thoughts to print. As I enjoy talking and Geoff enjoys writing, it was the perfect combination.

PHOTOGRAPHIC ACKNOWLEDGEMENTS

For permission to reproduce copyright photographs, the publishers would like to thank Mike Brett Photography and Colorsport

Captain's Log

My great pal, Bill Beaumont, wouldn't knowingly harm a fly but, when he was sadly forced to retire from the game early in 1982, he pitched me into a topsy-turvy period that I find hard to believe unless I study the statistics in black and white.

When that best-loved character in English rugby discovered a brain and then damaged it, I received the highest accolade by being invited to lead my country on the rugby union field. What happened to me thereafter, however, was hard to accept even for a player like myself, whose career has had more peaks and troughs than a roller coaster ride – a career, I might add, that isn't over yet; but I suppose the realization you might be into the twilight zone comes when a publisher invites you to pen your autobiography.

It was this very exercise that caused me to look back over a time that has been varied, to say the very least, filled with both memories to savour and memories best forgotten. I have been able to recall a career that has taken me around the globe, earned me a record number of international caps for an English scrum half, afford me the elation of historic victory and the despair of humiliating defeat, and caused me to suffer disappointments and frustrations inflicted by those who sit in judgement on a player's worth.

With the benefit of hindsight I might well have done some things differently but I have few personal regrets. I soon came to realize that even in an amateur game like rugby union no player is the master of his own destiny. For one thing there is a reliance on those around you and for another, the selectors have their role to play too.

Although I had a somewhat chequered career at selectorial hands, I still find it hard to credit the things that happened to me after Bill Beaumont retired from the game, when I was elevated to the England captaincy back in February 1982. I was to experience joy, success, failure, heartache and pressure to a degree I had never imagined.

So, before we embark together on a journey that I sincerely hope you will find interesting, revealing and entertaining, let me open the pages of my diary covering the period to which I have just referred. Had I not logged it in chronological order I doubt if anyone would believe it.

Saturday 30 January 1982

Good and bad news. Lancashire beat North Midlands in county championship final but we lost our skipper Bill Beaumont. Front five forwards don't have brains but Billy found one and damaged it!

Monday 1 February 1982

Arrived late at England squad session at Stourbridge. Cornered by chairman of selectors Budge Rogers. Thought I was in for a rollicking but what a shock instead. I'm to lead England against Ireland – talk about poacher turned gamekeeper and I'll bet a few England committee men will have heart attacks tomorrow.

Friday 5 February 1982

Now I know why Billy has a cauliflower ear. Its not through scrummaging but from the earache he gets from the press.

Saturday 6 February 1982

Lost by a point to Irish and played badly. Press conference afterwards was horrific and wonder how Bill coped all these years. Hope he's OK for next game although enjoyed captain's compensation – a suite at the Hilton after the game.

Friday 19 February 1982

Leading England against France at Parc des Princes tomorrow. This time it's for real because Bill has retired and the pressure is on me. If we lose I think my head will be first to roll. Such is life!

Saturday 20 February 1982
We won. Great feeling to thrash the French and we took it out on Paris with a vengeance although Colin Smart downed a bottle of aftershave and spent night in hospital.
Monday 22 February 1982
Smarty recovering and smells divine when he opens his mouth. 'Phone hasn't stopped ringing so I've taken it off the hook. How fickle folk are as I've suddenly switched from villain to hero.
Monday 8 March 1982
Still hung over from beating Welsh at Twickenham on Saturday. RFU treasurer told me my room bill at Hilton almost hit the £2000 mark. Thank goodness I don't have to pay. Great feeling to lead a winning England side and with summer trips to Bermuda, America and South Africa life could be a lot worse.
Monday 21 June 1982
Jet-lagged but happy. Clean sweep in England's tour of Canada and America. Lads played hard on and off field and morale is sky-high.
Saturday 16 October 1982
Thrashed Fiji 60–19 but people seemed more concerned with Adidas boot scandal than team's form. Stories flying around that the lads are being paid for wearing the company's boots and we were all looking over our shoulders for camera crews and aggrieved RFU officials. Instead of Adidas rep walking around with a white paintbrush enhancing the three stripes, we had RFU Secretary Bob Weighill going round with a marker pen blacking them out.
Friday 14 January 1983
We beat the Rest 47–7 in the trial this time but tomorrow's game against France worries me. Typical French philosophy in selection. Five or six really big 'nasties' and then eight or nine 'softies'. All the 'softies' can do 100 yards in about six seconds. If we get through 'nasties' we have a chance. If not...
Saturday 15 January 1983
Lost both Maurice Colclough and the game but no

complaints. France look title material again.

Monday 7 February 1983

Press gave us no chance against Wales at Cardiff Arms Park on Saturday but we drew 13–13. I was pleased with performance but press showered us in general, and me in particular, with a lot of harsh criticism. Oh well. It's happened before and confidence is high for the Scottish match.

Monday 21 February 1983

Budge called and before his 10p ran out he told me I was dropped from both the side and the squad. Felt my mere presence might be embarrassing. Ten minutes later RFU official Don Rutherford called, checking Budge had done his duty.

Monday 28 February 1983

Pleasantly intoxicated in Manchester nightclub when journalist friend called. My England replacement, Nigel Melville, had limped out of England training.

Tuesday 1 March 1983

Budge called. I'm playing against Scotland after all.

Monday 7 March 1983

We were beaten by Scotland. I'm relegated to replacement for Irish match and Budge and I exchange pleasantries in the newspaper columns. Must be some sort of record, after being captain on 5 February to have been dropped twice by 7 March. That means it's goodbye to any hope of a British Lions tour to New Zealand.

Monday 27 June 1983

On an aircraft en route to New Zealand. Surprise of all surprises. Terry Holmes is injured and now his replacement Nigel Melville is out of action so I'm on my travels again.

Wednesday 6 July 1983

Played my first game for the British Lions today ... as captain. Just to make my day complete we beat Hawkes Bay 25–19. I can't believe all that has happened to me in the last few months but, one way or another, there's not much new that can happen to me now.

1

In the Beginning (1951–69)

When I emerged, noisily, into an unsuspecting world, I wonder if my poor mother realized just how much of a handful she had given birth to.

She assures me now that I have given her enormous pleasure over the years but I'm sure that since the day in question, in July 1951, I must also have been a source of worry and bewilderment, due to my capacity for getting into scrapes or honest-to-goodness controversy.

This particular pilgrim's progress has tended to be eventful, whether breaking windows, ducking homework, getting picked and dropped, jetting off at the drop of an airline ticket, flashing my Burt Lancaster smile at the TV cameras or merely adding my two pennyworth to liven the pages of the popular newspapers we wrapped our fish and chips in before the invention of polystyrene trays.

It would be fair to say we have kept each other on our toes ever since because she and I are the half of the family that has lived up to the redhead reputation. Neither of us ever needed an invitation to leap in and have our say. Dad, God bless him, and my sister, Susan, are the quiet, calm, easy-going half of the family and they grew accustomed to sitting back to watch me sparring with an equally determined Mum. That's when I discovered the hard way that you win some, you lose some – valuable preparation for my international rugby career.

Not that rugby was ever discussed in those early days and certainly not at 1 Bowdon Street, Edgeley, Stockport, where I was born and which had been home for my mother throughout her life. It was from there she took me on my first sporting excursions, in my pram to the local park where she played hockey for a local works' team. I still have vague recollections of watching hockey from the confines of my baby carriage and it was probably from my mother that I inherited my ball skills. Dad was a good gymnast but is the first to admit that he and ball games went together like a round peg and a square hole.

The same has to be said of Susan, who was so uncoordinated she even had great difficulty clapping her hands together. She was the bookworm in the family and was a constant source of worry to my mother who couldn't get her out of the house. Needless to say, young Steven James Smith posed a problem of a different kind. She couldn't get him in!

I don't really recall anything of my first home because the four of us moved when I was two to a new council estate being built at Poynton. A move that very definitely placed us in the 'posh' category in the eyes of the remainder of the Smith clan – Dad was one of ten children – as Poynton, in those days, was little more than a pleasant village in the Cheshire countryside. And a far cry from the back streets of Stockport. The move was perfect for me because Poynton was a marvellously healthy place in which to grow up, surrounded as we were by open countryside.

Most of the people who moved into the new houses on the estate were of a similar age to my parents and that meant there was a large number of young children. That situation produced its share of gang warfare but, in times of peace, it was always easy to organize soccer and cricket teams. The streets became our playground and it was a world of Cup Finals and Test matches, with S. J. Smith in the thick of it. During the winter months we would kick a football around from dawn to dusk and summer was dominated by cricket with a dustbin serving as the wickets. Those were immensely happy days of six and out, and all out if the ball landed in the Jones's garden. One set of neighbours cut us dead for twenty years because my sister failed to hold my attempted cover drive. I always did have difficulty keeping them on the deck and that particular effort sailed straight through their window, showering their spanking new carpet, their *pièce de résistance*, with glass.

There must have been many times when my parents fervently wished I had been a bookworm like my sister, but I was intent on expeditions of discovery, diversions that were made all the more exciting because the estate was still being built. I seemed to spend most of my time in and out of workmen's shelters; the only time I was ever white was the day I fell into the lime pit. Everything the workmen did seemed to be exciting, so I quickly adopted a few of their practices. Not that the family were too pleased when I picked up the habit of swilling tea dregs around my cup before tossing them onto the lounge carpet. That produced a clip round the earhole, and my idea of cleaning out a cup was about as much appreciated as my use of Anglo-Saxon English one day when I was having some difficulty threading a lace into my pumps when I was in a hurry. The words, whatever they were, seemed appropriate for a moment of frustration because it was an expression of annoyance used by the workmen when they hammered their thumbs instead of a nail. Mother descended on me with a bar of soap and threatened to wash my mouth out with it.

The start of my schooldays must have come as a real blessing for her, although I wasn't particularly overjoyed at the thought of being incarcerated for nearly seven hours every day. It was only once I was there that I realized I was being given a licence to pursue my sole interest ... sport.

Poynton Primary School was a cracking educational establishment and I had a very happy time within its confines, especially when I was made captain of the school soccer team. As I was also captain of the Cubs team and the Woodford Community Centre team, life

13

was rather hectic for my parents who had the task of rushing me around the neighbourhood from one game to the next. The school used to announce the team every Friday and you really thought you had arrived in the big time if you were one of the chosen few swaggering out of school that afternoon with a school football jersey slung over your shoulder. We played in Blackburn Rovers colours and they were very prized items. I probably slept in mine, which was something of a habit with me. I slept in the cap when I was awarded my school colours at grammar school.

It was during all this sporting activity that a trait that has been with me ever since started to manifest itself. I became terribly competitive and a bad loser. I hate losing at anything; even street-corner marbles was high-pressure stuff for me. One year we lost a Cubs final at soccer and I remember marching round to the chief scoutmaster's house to protest and demand a replay.

I had to try to win everything. When we went on holiday, beach games could end up in fisticuffs. At home poor Susan had to spend hours bowling to me or letting me dribble around her, but on holiday I usually had my cousin Phillip to plague the life out of. He wasn't terribly sporty and I must have given him a hard time by hogging the ball, or bat, depending on which game we were playing. Phillip's sister and parents also had red hair, and each family had a motorcycle and sidecar. As we all set off on holiday we must have looked a bonny sight with those eight red heads bobbing about.

My competitive edge wasn't just associated with sport. When everyone else seemed to be joining the school choir, that became another challenge for me. In any sport I could invariably hold my place, but the choirmaster soon realized there was something wrong with my singing. In a bid to reach the source of the problem he kept dividing the choir until he found the culprit ... and kicked me out. I've never been able to sing a note but I couldn't bear not being involved with the rest of my schoolmates.

The crucial sphere of competition was the eleven-plus and I hardly needed motivation for that because Susan, who is a couple of years older than me, passed with flying colours. Determined not to be outdone, in 1962 I won a place at King's School, Macclesfield. Having achieved my goal, I immediately started having misgivings about it. First, it meant parting company with my friends at home and, secondly, the school played rugby instead of soccer. Rugby was a game I knew absolutely nothing about except that it was played with an oddly shaped ball. It amazed me that you needed brains to get to grammar school in order to get them kicked out again playing rugby.

King's was, and still is, a fantastic school for sport and I soon grew accustomed to playing with an oval ball. Enthusiasm for the game was immediate. We used to hire a ball for a penny at lunchtime and spend hours kicking it over the posts. I did a great deal of kicking in my early days and it was only at Loughborough that I stopped dead-ball kicking because it put an extra strain on my problematic hamstrings. Despite my obvious affiliation to soccer there was no resistance on my part to playing rugby, except when I was picked for the Under 12s on a Saturday when I wanted to play for a local soccer side. The headmaster, hearing of my protest, called me into his study. Mr T. T. Shaw then proceeded to tell me, in no uncertain terms, that I would be playing for the school team.

Initially, the school tried to turn me into a forward, but I took one look at what went on in the scrum and said I wasn't having any of that, thank you very much. I suspect as a form of punishment I was put on the wing where I became King's answer to Billy Boston. It was whilst languishing in that position that I first met a little scrum half from Cowley School, St Helens. His name was John Horton and neither of us could possibly have imagined then that we would partner each other in an England Grand Slam side.

We were still learning the laws of what seemed, to a

15

young schoolboy, a terribly complex game, and when Johnny suddenly called for a mark, we all stopped playing because we thought he must have hurt himself to cry out like that. The referee didn't allow the mark so the little devil raced off and scored a try under our posts. He gave a fantastic display of rugby that day and it was the first time I had ever seen anyone sidestep. We must have done an awful lot of standing back and admiring because Cowley thrashed us by 40 points. We were clearly fast learners though. We returned later that season and beat them.

I have a feeling I had graduated to scrum half by that time, so Johnny and I would have been in direct opposition. Later he switched to fly half.

Our Under-12s scrum half couldn't pass a ball and would spend the whole game kicking it into the box. That wasn't much fun for a winger, but I managed to get into the action by virtue of the fact that wingers at that time used to throw the ball in at lineouts. I worked out a move with our hooker and when we played against Stockport Grammar School I threw the ball directly to him at the front of the line. He immediately threw it back to me and I dive-passed out to the fly half, missing out the poor old scrum half. One of the masters took note and my scrum half career started with the next game. But for that one piece of initiative I might never have switched to the position that best suited my physique and temperament. Once established in my new role, I was fortunate in having a dedicated rugby coach in Dai Jones, a fanatical Welshman, who had a tremendous influence on me in my formative rugby years.

Cricket, however, was still my first love and that occupied the rest of my time, along with soccer and three newspaper rounds. By doing three rounds I received three wages, the only disadvantage being to have to stagger around three separate estates with three bags over my shoulders. It's a wonder I ever found time to study. It took me slightly longer to break through in rugby, compared with cricket. At the tender age of thirteen I was made a subprefect – a distinction given to house captains – and by that time I was captain of my house cricket team. So I was really taking off in a sporting sense, but I never did get higher than subprefect!

It was in cricket that I started playing alongside men at an early age. I was a member of the Woodford senior team and many a pace bowler must have wondered about the little sprog of a lad, only just out of short pants, opening the innings for the first team. If they thought I was too small to drive the ball back over their heads they were probably right, but I became a dab hand at scoring boundaries behind the wicket. That technique helped me to hit enough big scores to top the batting averages at the age of fourteen. As I was also playing for the school first team and for Cheshire Schools, I had greater expectations of reaching the top as a cricketer. My one great disappointment came when I just failed to make the England Schools side. The opener in possession stayed on for a third year in the sixth form at Hipperholme Grammar School and my chance went out of the window.

On the rugby front, I got into the Cheshire Schools side in the 1965/66 season and advanced to the North of England trials where I came face to face with Johnny Horton again. He was established as the big star of the Lancashire Schools side but I jumped all over him that afternoon. It was pouring with rain and every time he tried to sidestep he landed on his backside. By that stage I had developed a good pass and the selectors went for me, rather than Johnny, when they picked the next trial teams. We played in the Midlands; I felt I had played well and other people kept telling me I had done so, but I failed to make the final England trial. What with the cricket situation as well, it looked as though I would never represent my country. For some odd reason, I only thought in terms of playing for England as a schoolboy.

I had developed a long spin pass as a result of watching Chris Laidlaw on television. I decided that he was the player to copy and immediately misappropriated my mother's yard brush and stuck it up in the garden to use as a marker, aiming to hit it every time whilst passing from farther and farther away.

Around that time I started to see how my future might unfold once I had left school. I was invited to join a Cheshire Schools rugby coaching course, at which one of the coaches was Gerald Davies. I hadn't a clue who he was and nearly fell out of my chair soon afterwards when I saw him running in tries for Wales on television. The course really fired my enthusiasm and I decided I wanted to go on to study at Loughborough College, even if only to get my hands on one of their African violet tracksuits!

The thought of teaching sport appealed to me and, over the years, I have always enjoyed working with youngsters and passing on my experience. It can be very rewarding. If at all possible I never turn down a coaching session with children because I am aware of how much I was influenced by the sessions I attended. For that reason I hope mini rugby proves successful. The concept is marvellous, although some of the parents may destroy it if we aren't very careful. There is nothing worse than fanatical parents screaming from the touchline.

My father always came to watch me playing sport, but he would stay in the background. You only knew he was there because you could see the motorcycle combination parked alongside the Jags and Rovers. His support was of the best kind. We were never a wealthy family by any stretch of the imagination, but whenever I needed sports gear it was provided without question. He always gave me a lot of encouragement and even now he attends practically every match I play. But to push himself forward or bellow from the touchline would be anathema to him.

There was an unsavoury incident involving mini rugby when I was playing for Sale in the Glengarth Sevens, a very commendable annual tournament which raises money for mentally handicapped children. Sale had reached the final (in fact we won the event that year) and the players were in the dressing room before the game when a group of parents came in with their children who were to play in a time-filler between the semis and the final. They tried to kick us out to make way for their young protégés. When I reminded them that we had played in several hard rounds already and were due to play in the final shortly, I was told belligerently, 'We know who you are, big head. Now get out because the kids are coming in here.'

Needless to say, that little group were ignominiously thrown out, but the irony was that I was then asked to present the medals to the mini players. I felt sorry for the boys because all their parents did was scream like banshees from the touchline. Mini rugby would be great without that type of parent.

Other sports had started to occupy my time at school. At one stage I was representing King's at basketball, squash, rugby and cricket. I won the school squash cup three years on the run, the first time, at the age of fifteen, as a rank outsider, only recently having taken up the game. The only coaching I had received was someone telling me to dominate the T, which I did. Of course, all this sporting activity didn't exactly assist me academically and when I stepped up to receive the trophy, an ordeal in itself, the headmaster leaned forward and whispered that he wished my work was of the same standard as my sporting activity.

What with my newspaper rounds and umpteen training sessions every week for a variety of sports, I never seemed to have time to study. When the O-levels came around, however, I was in for a rude awakening. Mum, concerned that I was doomed to fail, placed a total ban on sporting activity. I couldn't believe it and, being me, didn't take it lying down. I kicked up a great fuss and there were times when I could see Dad starting to weaken. But Mum stuck to her guns. It was one battle I very definitely lost. Yet, whilst I certainly didn't appreciate it at the time, it was that period of discipline that enabled me to achieve my ambition of going on to Loughborough.

Once the ban was lifted the frenzy of sporting activity continued as before. Somehow I found time to play soccer for the Stockport and District youth team and even cherished an ambition of playing for Manchester United. I was United daft and would take a defeat so personally that I wouldn't speak to anybody.

Although I played rugby at school on Saturday mornings, I used to turn out for Stockport at soccer on Sundays. When we reached the semifinals of the Cheshire Youth Cup in March 1968 we were drawn against Macclesfield and I decided not to tell my pals at school who hated rugby but were crazy about soccer. What a surprise I had when I rolled up at the Moss Rose ground, Macclesfield, with my boots over my arm. Nearly all of them were playing for the opposition. One of my great schoolfriends who played against me that day was Steve Pearson, the son of former United player, Stan Pearson. Steve was a good footballer but also proved a dab hand on the tennis courts too and went on to play tennis for Cheshire.

Stockport won that game 2–1 and advanced to the final, an occasion which helped persuade me that Rugby Union was a far better game to be involved in socially. After the game both sides were invited to a reception at Stockport Town Hall, but only one player from our team and I actually turned up. We had lost and the rest of the lads had gone straight home.

By now I had started to sample senior rugby and discovered to my delight that Rugby Union offered a very different scenario. Macclesfield rugby club falls into the 'very sociable' bracket and, typically, once you start playing with men – as I was at both rugby and cricket – you start doing everything else as well. I was duly introduced to beer and thought it the most horrible liquid to have ever passed my lips. Not that it took me long to acquire the taste. The seasoned Macclesfield

20

drinkers nursed me through my first few pints and I've done the brew fair justice ever since.

There was the inevitable embarrassing moment. Having discovered the drink that separates the men from the boys, I marched boldly up to the bar and asked for a pint. The barmaid asked if I wanted bitter or mild and I said, no, I wanted a pint of beer. That brought me out in the old red flush.

While I was in the sixth form I played rugby and cricket at school, cricket and soccer for Poynton and rugby for Macclesfield. After making an appearance for Macclesfield one weekend, I was delivering newspapers the next week when I spotted the first headline ever written about me. It said: 'Young Smith stars for Macclesfield'. I nearly dropped the paper. After recovering from the initial shock I sat down on a doorstep to read the article. I just wish they could have all been so complimentary.

Steve Midgelow, who later accompanied me to Loughborough, Wilmslow and Sale, became my close friend. He was talented at both cricket and rugby, but although he went on to play senior county rugby with Cheshire, he had to quit the game early because of recurring injury problems. Midge and I spent so many hours hitching lifts home from rugby clubs, cricket clubs, soccer matches and training sessions that it's a miracle we ever got our A-levels to earn places at Loughborough. But we did, and felt ready for whatever college life had to offer.

My childhood had been almost totally dominated by sport and my parents must have been thankful they had somehow managed to steer me through the academic system and into the environment I wanted. Goodness knows what I would have done if I hadn't gone to Loughborough. One thing is certain, I might never have played for England and that is something I wouldn't have missed for anything. But, as I journeyed to Loughborough, the possibility of playing senior rugby for England still hadn't really occurred to me.

21

2

Cotton, College and Coaching
(1969–72)

Going to Loughborough was like starting out on a great adventure ... and that's exactly how it worked out. It marked one of the turning points of my life and, when I look back, the three years I spent there seem as fantastic now as they did at the time.

Like most other youngsters who go on to college, this was my first real break with family and home. I remember standing in the room I had been allocated and thinking to myself that this was it. Independence. The situation looked decidedly rosy. I had just opened my first bank account, there was a bar fifty yards away and the tower block next door housed two hundred women. I may still have been slightly damp behind the ears but it didn't take me long to catch on!

It didn't take me long to achieve my great ambition either, to possess one of the college tracksuits. It meant so much to me that I slept in it the first night, just like when I got my first school cap.

Getting involved in the rugby scene straight away was ideal and it also introduced me to a marvellous social life. There was something of a surprise in store for me, however, because I had mistakenly thought I was somebody, having played rugby for Cheshire School-boys. The rude awakening came at the Freshers' trial – there were another eight county schoolboy scrum halves in competition for a first-team place. Just for good measure, the college also had seven senior county fullbacks. The array and depth of rugby talent was unbelievable and, with Stu Winship of Harlequins playing scrum half for the college first team, I had to settle for captaincy of the Freshers.

At the time the first team included players like John Gray, who went on to hook for England at different levels; Ray Hughes, who played for England at Under-25 level before turning to Rugby League with St Helens; Des Diamond, who got a final England trial; and David Cooke, who went one better and got a cap. Keith Fielding was on the wing, and he was joined by Lewis Dick, the only Fresher to walk straight into the first team.

I was called in to play the occasional game but I had greater success when the cricket season came around and I found myself batting at four for the First XI. The cricketing talent was equally as impressive as that in other sporting spheres at the college and nine of the side had played for MCC Schools. They included Tony Borrington, who went on to play for Derbyshire, Geoff Tolchard (Roger's brother), Alan Hampshire (John's brother), Tony Mottram, the Hampshire fast bowler and, of course, the inevitable John Gray. The following season we were joined by Graham Barlow.

The player who impressed me most was John Gray. He is still the greatest all-round sportsman I have ever met. He had played soccer for Coventry Schools and had played hardly any rugby until he arrived at Lough-borough. Yet, within three years, he had played county rugby and been on an England tour. John had played cricket for MCC Schools and was a Warwickshire fast bowler. As if that wasn't enough, John was also a great athlete and highly competitive. It is significant that he went on a Great Britain Rugby League tour within eighteen months of turning professional. That was a tremendous achievement when you consider how difficult it is for a forward to switch codes.

Playing for the Freshers proved an enjoyable experience, especially when we discovered the delights of playing away. The college had two sides which were considered to be equal in terms of playing strength, the Freshers and the Collegiates, and they alternated between playing at home and away. On our first two away trips we had such a great time that we volunteered to do the travelling every week. These outings turned into marvellous student expeditions of rape and pillage – not literally, of course – but our bubble had to burst eventually. One of the lads drafted into the side as a reserve hooker happened to be a divinity student. What we regarded as typical student high jinks obviously jarred his sensibilities and he 'snitched' on us.

We were soon back playing alternate weeks at home but that didn't really matter because Loughborough was proving the ideal introduction to life in general and sport in particular. As a youngster, at a club like Macclesfield or Wilmslow, you were always regarded as a snotty-nosed kid by the men. But at Loughborough you were with your peers and that made a great difference.

Jim Greenwood was our coach and he was a fantastic influence. Quite apart from fitness training and tactical coaching, Jim also took us for English. He would walk into a lecture clutching a photostat copy of two lines from a poem by Milton and proceed to talk nonstop for forty minutes about life, using the two lines as his theme. All the tearaway, reckless PE students were totally trans-fixed and went away thinking seriously about their lives and careers. It was such a big influence on one of our year that he left the college after Jim had delivered a powerful oration during which he asked if we really wanted to be at Loughborough. The poor lad took it completely to heart.

During the summer prior to my third year at Lough-borough, Jim had been reading the thoughts of Chair-man Mao. For the whole of that season the team sheet went up on the notice board accompanied by the thought Jim considered most appropriate.

He couldn't possibly have had a more captivated or motivated bunch of young maniacs to work with. We would have run through a brick wall for him. The college's approach was very professional, with regular training, tactical talks before games and debriefing sessions once the dust had settled.

We worked hard at our rugby but we played hard as well. Our major 'thrash' of the week used to be on a Friday night when most self-respecting rugby players were having a couple of quiet beers and going to bed early. However, we were all young and naturally fit. In more recent times I have had to pace myself rather differently!

My second year at Loughborough was when things started to happen and a major influence came into my life. At the start of term I was more or less earmarked for the first-team scrum-half berth, having played quite well on my occasional outings the previous season. The only obstacle on the horizon was a new arrival that term – Brynmor Williams. Brynmor had been written up as the most capped Welsh schoolboy who was destined to become the second Gareth Edwards. It was one hell of a challenge but I won the vote after playing against him in the trial. Luckily, from my point of view, he got a bit homesick and went back to Wales, leaving me free to enjoy two fantastic seasons.

The major influence came over the horizon, blotting out the sun in the process. The first-team squad had arrived back at college a week early and we were joined by the Freshers. We were all out on the track for a typical Greenwood session and were wearing our African violet tracksuits, running vests, trainers – all the latest gear as befits young thoroughbreds. Suddenly, a lumbering giant came lolloping over the hill towards us, with a quiff, a pair of sideburns, great flared shorts and a pair of Woollies pumps on his feet. Fran Cotton had arrived.

We had heard that one of the new students would be a prop forward from Liverpool who had played for Lanca-shire. It was the general view that he might be a useful acquisition ... but we couldn't believe our eyes when we first saw him.

The session that followed was a real killer. Sprints, 400 and 800 metres in quick succession. We reckoned the new boy was really going to bite the dust. By the end of the session we were dying, but were staggered to find that big Fran had kept up with us.

In the showers afterwards I had some soap in my eyes and as I tried to restore my vision I quipped to my pal, Steve Watkins, 'Have you seen the chin on that Fran Cotton. If you turned him upside down you could plough the first team pitch with him.' Guess who was standing right behind me?

Anyway, the big feller took it well and my admiration for him started to grow. He walked straight into the first team and played a significant role in our first match, which was against Staffordshire who had won the county title the previous season. Their side included Mike Davis, who later coached England, Welshman Terry Cobner, the late Sam Doble and the player destined to become my sparring partner later, Jan Webster.

We drew 12–12, which seemed a marvellous result until you looked at the talent in the Loughborough side. Fran and John Gray were in the front row, Dick Cowman was at fly half, Des Diamond and David Cooke were in the centre, Lewis Dick and Clive Rees (who arrived when Keith Fielding left) were on the wings, and Phil Jenkins, the Llanelli player, was at fullback.

The Fijians were touring England at the time and all the England selectors were at our game to check on form. Having only played about five first-team games I hadn't even heard of selectors but they must have been impressed because Fran and John were picked for the England Under-25s to play Fiji and I was on the bench.

Before that little outing we had to entertain the Metropolitan Police and that was regarded as the college's punch-up game. It was a case of the 'big, nasty, coppers' heading north to sort out the poor little students. It was a fixture nobody really relished but what a surprise they were in for that year. The students had flocked onto the hill to watch the contest. When I bent

down to pop the ball into the first scrum, it suddenly
erupted and Fran, who had apparently been gouged,
stood up and wiped out their entire front row with three
punches. The students went mad, wading into the police
as they beat a hasty retreat. Nobody had ever seen
anything like it at Loughborough before. We were, after
all, the ones to be bullied by bigger and older sides but
we realized for the first time that nobody was going to
bully us that season.

I was beginning to see F. E. Cotton in a new light and
he had yet another surprise up his sleeve. He had an old
VW car, which he called Dobbin, and when we drove
down to London for the Fijian match it got a flat tyre.
After unscrewing the wheel nuts Fran simply lifted the
car off the ground whilst I feverishly changed the wheel.
I had only known the bloke for about a week and a half
but I was already quite impressed with him!

I'll never forget that weekend. Not only were we
training with the gods of the day, Dave Duckham and
John Spencer, we were also sampling something of the
international atmosphere for the first time. We met for a
training session at Esher on the Thursday before the
game and I watched Jacko Page, who had been chosen at
scrum half, throwing out a few passes to Ian Wright.
Then it was my turn and, although I was rather nervous,
I thought it went quite well as I passed off both hands to
the fly half. At that stage, Dickie Jeeps – whom I didn't
know from Adam – turned to me and said something
like, 'You scrum halves these days ought to get on your
belly and dive-pass.'

That comment, I might tell you, left me full of
confidence. It was my first meeting with an England
selector and I hadn't the faintest idea who he was.
Another selector, Eric Evans, was from my own part of
the country and I didn't know him either. Coming as I
had from a mainly soccer background, I hadn't met any
past players.

My services weren't needed during the game but I
remember sitting next to Peter Wheeler on the replace-

27

ments' bench. We've both seen a bit of service together since then but at that first meeting he looked too angelic to be a hooker. I decided he must be a fly half!

My lack of a rugby background posed another problem after the game. I was told I would need a dinner jacket for the banquet that evening. I didn't even know what a dinner jacket was, let alone possess one. John Bone, who later coached Cheshire, saved the day by lending me his. He was an ex-public schoolboy so he would have a DJ, wouldn't he? Unfortunately, the suit was about five times too big.

It was that season my playing career also took off in another direction. Steve Midgelow and I were called up to Wilmslow to play for the Rest in the senior Cheshire trial. With John Lansbury as captain, we smashed Cheshire 24–6 and afterwards, while I was hanging around the bar waiting for the side to be announced, the selectors called me into their room to tell me I was Cheshire's new captain.

Looking back, it seems unbelievable that after a handful of games at senior level, in the space of a month I had been on an England weekend, drawn with the county champions and been appointed captain of Cheshire. I was just nineteen.

When I got back to college, Jim Greenwood couldn't believe it. I suspect the same went for most of the team and I was just thankful Midge had been picked as my halfback partner. At least we knew one another! The only other player I knew, and then only by reputation, was Peter Stagg from Sale, the most famous name in the squad.

The funny thing was that we were into coaching in a big way at Loughborough but I hadn't realized that coaching had yet to be born in most of the outside world. We were cocooned into thinking that what we were doing was the norm. It was difficult for us to appreciate that outside our sport-crazy environment people were doing the odd lap or two, having a few pints and going home. At the Cheshire sessions there was no emphasis on coaching and there I was, a little sprat, trying to get the lads organized. They stared at me as though I was some kind of idiot. Staggy looked down at me from about 6 feet 11 inches, probably wondering who this little brat from Loughborough thought he was, trying to tell a man with nearly thirty Scottish caps and a Lions tour behind him how to play rugby.

Jim Greenwood had a long chat with me the night before the first game against Durham. He told me to try to give some kind of team talk, to think about the game and how it should be played. Needless to say, the lad later dubbed the Cheshire Cat was as nervous as a kitten.

When the time for the team talk came I tried to convey how I wanted the side to approach the game. Then I noticed that Peter Stagg had fallen asleep in the corner of the dressing room. I thought I had better shut up and get on with the warm-up session instead. I launched myself into this massively vigorous warm-up – typical Lough-borough head-banging stuff that had you perspiring nicely before you even reached the field of combat – and suddenly realized that only Midge was doing it with me. Thirteen sets of eyeballs were staring at two lunatics going mad in a corner.

Trotting out on to the field was a relief, and it was an even bigger relief for the young skipper when Cheshire thrashed Durham 38–3. The New Brighton winger Peter Welton grabbed a hat trick of tries and Midge produced a fine solo effort to add to his four conversions and a penalty.

The next big shock came as I was sitting down enjoying my meal at the reception and slipping a few beers down my throat. My reverie was shattered when someone called upon the Cheshire captain to reply to a toast. Nobody had bothered to tell me I was expected to make a speech. It's the only time in my life that I've been lost for words. I ended up saying something, but I can't for the life of me remember what.

By Cheshire standards 1970–71 was a reasonable season, although the results were fairly typical. We beat

Durham and Cumbria, had a good game with Lancashire, ran Yorkshire quite close and got hammered by
Northumberland.

The success rate at Loughborough was a good deal
higher. We had a close shave against Durham in the
quarter finals of the UAU Championship, but went on
to beat Bangor to earn a meeting with Nottingham in
what became the first UAU final at Twickenham.
Nottingham held us until half time but we proved too
strong after the break, with Des Diamond, Dave Jackson
and Lewis Dick scoring tries and Dick Cowman kicking
goals to give us a 22–3 victory. It was a fitting highlight
to a great college year which also saw me attending my
first senior England squad session.

The lasting impression I had of that weekend was of a
bloke who seemed about 7 feet tall, smoking a cigarette
whilst trying to fasten his bootlaces. He was coughing
and wheezing and looked as though he didn't have long
for this world. It was my introduction to Chris Ralston!

I finished off my second year at Loughborough by
getting into the cricket First XI again. Then, at the end
of term, with a couple of mates I followed the well-worn
student trail to Greece. Six weeks later I was back in
England tanned and a good deal slimmer than when I
left. Typical students, we soon ran short of funds in
Greece and ended up selling our blood to raise a few bob
to buy food and beer. We seemed to spend half the
holiday with the down-and-outs at the Athens blood
bank.

So, it was a lean, brown, mean and keen Smithy who
returned to Loughborough in 1971 to begin his final
year. John Gray had left and Fran was appointed
captain, with myself as his deputy.

We were keen to do well, so I opted out of the Cheshire
captaincy because there was too much travelling involved to attend all the sessions. Mind you, I had good
company on my frequent trips home in the shape of
Fran, who was training with Lancashire.

By that stage we had become great pals, but I

discovered something of Fran's hard mental attitude to the game when we played against each other in a Cheshire v. Lancashire match. By coincidence, both team coaches arrived at the ground together. Quite naturally, I said Hello to Fran, cheerful chap that I am. To my amazement, my big buddy stalked straight past, totally ignoring me. It was then I thought, Hello, there's a bit of a game coming up here.

Despite our valiant efforts Loughborough didn't reach the UAU final that season, but Wilmslow presented me with the chance to further my international claims. The Cheshire Club was involved in the new national knock-out cup competition – now the John Player Cup – and I travelled over with Midge to play for them.

In the first round we beat Liverpool, then followed up with a win over Birkenhead Park and found ourselves drawn away to Harlequins in the quarter finals. That had to be the biggest game Wilmslow had ever been involved in and nobody really gave us a chance. We were virtually unheard of and Harlequins had a side bursting with talent. The odds against us were understandable when you consider that the opposition included Bob Lloyd, David Cooke, Mike Davis, Peter Dixon and Nigel Starmer-Smith.

The weather had been terrible and the pitch was something of a mudbath. By the end of the afternoon we were being hailed as the 'Mighty Mudlarks', having beaten them 16–7. Our handling in the conditions was quite remarkable and we also adapted to the conditions far better than Quins. Two of our tries came when the ball was hacked through the mud by Jim Barker and Gareth Jones.

That was also the first and only time I have played against Nigel. The following day one of the newspapers said that the single-barrelled Smith had outplayed the double-barrelled Smith.

Wilmslow had to travel to Moseley in the semifinals. We held the Midlanders fairly well but they galloped away a bit towards the end. But we put the icing on the cake by winning the Cheshire Cup to make 1971–72 Wilmslow's most memorable season.

With the rugby season over I settled into cricket again, and, as this was my final year, there was a frantic round of parties. But my socializing came to an abrupt halt when I was called up as a replacement for England in South Africa, my first representative rugby tour abroad. That role was to become something of a habit!

3

Boks, Blacks and Ba-Bas
(1972)

When the RFU sent me a reserve card for England's
tour to South Africa in the summer of 1972, I was still
sufficiently new to the international scene to be unsure
about whether I was the only reserve or one of many.
Needless to say, my college friends indulged in a fair
amount of kidology, with the result that when the call
came I didn't believe it.

Lionel Weston had been injured and my country
needed me. It was left to Jim Greenwood to drag me out
of a lecture and convince me that the call was for real. I
was to tally unprepared for a sudden departure. A trip to
somewhere as far away as South Africa was something I
couldn't comprehend.

Fortunately, Jim organized me. He even went to the
extreme of going out and buying me a washbag as my
idea of luggage was a toothbrush and a ticket. Steve
Midgelow lent me his blazer and flannels, another friend
chipped in with a shirt and somebody else gave me a tie.

By now I had become the proud owner of an old GPO
van, which I had painted in Loughborough colours, and
after piling my new aquisitions into it I raced back to
Poynton. I then had the task of trying to convince a
somewhat bewildered mother that her son really was
going off to play rugby in South Africa. At the same time
I was charging through the house like a whirlwind,
trying to get things together.

It was still a mesmerized young man who clambered

aboard the London train at Stockport station. The rain was pouring from a leaden sky and I was huddled up in a duffel coat. I was still wearing it when the flight from Heathrow arrived in South Africa where the temperature was in the eighties.

I was learning new things all the time – one being that you don't need a duffel coat in South Africa. The next thing I discovered was that rugby is taken rather more seriously in that part of the world, and that knowledge was added to my earlier realization that some rugby players have to wear dinner jackets and make speeches. Like the other passengers standing in the queue waiting to leave the airport, I was wondering which star had travelled with us. There were press photographers everywhere with their cameras at the ready. It never once occurred to me that I could be the focus of attention. That brought home immediately the importance of the game over there and why they are so desperate to keep their rugby link with the rest of the world.

A car whisked me off to the team's hotel and my feet settled back on terra firma when I met up with Fran again. I was so new to this level of rugby that Fran was the only member of the party I could seriously claim to know. There were one or two players in the England party to South Africa that I got to know rather better as the years rolled by. Players like Tony Neary and Mickey Burton, who became great touring companions, and Alan Old, whom I would like to have seen more of as a halfback partner.

With Alex Lewis as manager and John Elders as coach, it was a happy and successful tour and as I am extremely adaptable if nothing else, I slotted into touring with great ease. The day-to-day existence was a complete contrast to what I was used to. From a student environment, I was suddenly living in five-star hotels and being treated like a superstar. At that stage in my life it was the best thing that had ever happened to me. I thought I was in paradise.

Little did I realize at that stage that I was settling into what became a familiar pattern in the future – being called out at a moment's notice to sit on the replacements' bench. On that occasion I donned a senior England shirt for the first time and settled on the bench at Pretoria to watch the lads play against Northern Transvaal. Nero and Fran played in that game, John Pullin was captain and Jan Webster was at scrum half. It was a very hard game and at one stage the lads were 13–3 down, but they battled back to force a draw, thanks to a try by Andy Ripley and three penalty goals by Sam Doble.

That draw dented what would have been a 100 per cent record for the tour and would probably have ended in defeat had not Fran pulled off a marvellous try-saving cover tackle on one of the Northern Transvaal wingers just five yards from the England line. That was Loughborough fitness for you.

The only international of the tour was due to be played the following weekend in Johannesburg so I was drafted into the Tuesday side to play Griqualand West at Kimberley. It was very much the dirt-trackers' side but I had Alan Old to partner me and we were about to share in a little piece of rugby history making.

We swamped the opposition 60–21 and ran in nine tries into the bargain. But the highlight of the game was Alan Old's performance in setting a new British scoring record with 24 points. Over the years since I have seen him produce some marvellously accurate kicking but nothing could match his display that afternoon. He converted all the tries, dropped a goal and kicked a penalty. The tries were scored by John Spencer (two), Lancashire wing Tony Richards (two), Stack Stevens, John Watkins, Jeremy Janion, Alan Morley and Tim Cowell.

It was a real headline maker and the press got rather carried away the following day because they started picking me for the Test team. Admittedly, I felt I had played well but it would have been ludicrous to have pitched me straight into a Test match against South Africa. Common sense prevailed and Jan was picked to play instead. He responded to the pressure that had been put on him by playing an absolute blinder in a historic 18–9 victory.

Alan Old had certainly played his way into the side, but in the Test the kicking duties were taken over by Sam Doble who kicked four penalties and converted Alan Morley's try. It was another of those occasions when the England forwards produced the goods and I was impressed by Andy Ripley, who had an outstanding game in the middle of the back row.

I watched from the replacements' bench and, having played midweek, got in one more game on that tour than I managed with the British Lions when they called me up in 1980.

That tour was the first time I had played in really great heat. When I left the field at Kimberley I looked as though I had had a fit. I was frothing at the mouth and Fran was in stitches watching me try to drink a Coca-Cola. I was desperate for a drink but my mouth was so dry that I couldn't swallow.

By the time I arrived back in England I thought I really had made it. My last few weeks at Loughborough before going out into the big wide world turned into one long celebration. Even the cricket suffered.

Before leaving that sporting and academic haven – in addition to playing rugby and cricket I had also found time to study history – I had fixed myself up with a teaching job at a college in Cheshire. I had also arranged to move into a bungalow in Chester with an old pal of mine from my scouting days.

It was another total change of life and I was soon faced with another decision – whether or not to change my club. Although I had played most of my senior rugby at Loughborough my club experience during those three years had been with Wilmslow. I had enjoyed playing there and the side had proved itself in the John Player Cup. But people kept telling me to leave the club and join Sale in order to improve my chances.

At the time I found the situation very difficult. I didn't know anyone at Sale well and, as I had just been whisked away from my mates at Loughborough, Wilmslow had a certain attraction because I knew the other players. However, a player's chances of success at the top can only be enhanced by moving into the highest level of the game at club level.

But in 1972 I was unsure what to do and the pressure started to build up with a series of telephone calls from the old Sale warhorse, Dick Trickey, who was then captain. He wanted me to play at Sale and the telephone saga ended with me telling him I had decided to stay at Wilmslow. That went down like a lead balloon because he barked, 'I'll see you on the field then,' and slammed the phone down.

That was typical Dick. He could never stop competing ... even on the telephone. I came to realize over the years, though, what a great character he is and what a credit to the game he has been. After college I was amazed at the attitude of many senior players to training, but you could never fault Dick on that score. Training was food and drink to him.

Eventually I sat down and thought very seriously about what I ought to do. There was no disputing that Sale had a much stronger fixture list. Wilmslow were new boys on the senior scene whereas Sale had a lengthy tradition on their side and, as a result, played some of the best sides in the country on a regular basis. That meant that their fixture list had a more competitive edge to it. After thinking the whole thing through I decided to start the 1972–73 season in Sale colours.

In a way I was sad at leaving Wilmslow, especially when they beat Sale on the first occasion I turned out against my old club, but I was soon convinced I had made the right decision. Naturally, Wilmslow were upset about it at the time because I was on the verge of a full England cap and I suppose that would have been a wonderful boost for a club that did what Orrell have done so effectively in recent seasons, break through into the senior rankings. It probably didn't help when my pal Midge followed me down to Heywood Road.

By moving to Sale I was taking something of a gamble because there was no guarantee of a first-team place. When I arrived the regular scrum half was Alan Morritt, who played fairly regularly for Lancashire and was the club's vice-captain. The other thing in his favour was the fact that he was, and still is, a very popular member of the club. However, unlike my first year at Lough-borough, I didn't have to wait in the wings. I suppose I was moving quickly up the rugby ladder, nothing seemed to go wrong for me and I went straight into Sale's first team. It was then I joined forces with John Horton. It was nice to find myself on the same side for a change and we established a marvellous partnership until he moved to Bath.

My time with Sale has always been happy and I got off to a good start because they had a strong side, with Tricks as a captain who led by example. He was partnered in the second row by Peter Stagg, and with Alan Newall, John Lansbury and Henry Dale in the front row we had a front five capable of providing a good platform for a cheeky young scrum half on his way up.

Even so, I thought I had returned to the Stone Age in terms of preparation. Sale trained as hard as any club – inevitable with Tricks as captain – but there was never any coaching as I had known it at Loughborough. There was nobody to offer real advice, no serious discussion of tactics and certainly no debriefing sessions afterwards. Today, young players have so many advantages if they join a club with a good coaching set-up. Their problems can be analysed and sorted out. I'm sure my own career might have been rather different with the right sort of help at a time when my international career was in tatters.

That season, 1972–73, I got involved with Cheshire again and went along to the squad sessions before the county championship started. All that did was further convince me that outside Loughborough nobody seemed to know what they were doing. At one of our sessions we were introduced to a mystery character called 'Noddy' Slater who played for Old Birkonians, a Cheshire junior club which is now defunct. The idea was that he would captain and coach the side and play at prop. That turned out to be another inspired piece of Cheshire selection because he was pitted against my old mate Fran when we played Lancashire. Before the game Noddy told me quite confidently that he had played against Fran a number of times. What he didn't tell me was that he had played against Fran as a number 8!

Well, Fran was bad enough at the best of times, but when you put him in a Lancashire shirt he was meaner than usual. At only the second scrum Fran put Noddy to the test and it was no contest. Poor Noddy was on his way to the dressing room with damaged ribs.

I assume he went to the dressing room; but he wasn't in the dressing room when we left the field. He wasn't at the post-match dinner either and, to be honest, I don't know anyone who ever saw him again. He didn't just walk off the field; he walked out of our lives.

Selectors have a lot to answer for sometimes and I think that was one of them. Someone commented afterwards that Noddy had been quite a bit smaller than Fran. Hell, he was even smaller than me!

Cheshire were literally put through the mangle by Lancashire that afternoon and their scrum half, Wyn Williams, played a blinder behind a rampant pack. I had one eye on the North West Counties side to play Ian Kirkpatrick's All Blacks a few weeks later, but thought Wyn's performance had put paid to any chance I had of getting into the team. I shouldn't have worried, however. At that stage setbacks seemed impossible, it was only later that I was to experience the disappointment, frustration and, occasionally, anger at being overlooked. The hint that I might land the scrum-half berth was dropped very heavily when I was chosen to play for North West Counties in a warm-up game against

39

Midland Counties at Leicester. That outing clearly went all right so far as the selectors were concerned because I found myself preparing to fulfil any young player's dream by playing against the All Blacks.

John Burgess came into my life at that point, as coach to the North West Counties side. I had heard a lot about him and seen at close quarters what he had achieved with Lancashire. He seemed to be the only man in the north who was getting to grips with coaching as I understood it; it was largely through his efforts that Lancashire had become such a dominant force again. The sessions were so enjoyable it was like being back at Loughborough.

In those days the All Blacks seemed invincible. Nobody ever seemed to beat them, so it was a massive upset when Llanelli bettered them in 1972, the master plan having been drawn up by Carwyn James. That defeat seemed, on the face of it, to make our chances of success even slimmer because the tourists were likely to harden their resolve not to lose any more games.

We weren't exactly written up as the great English hopes by the press and the All Blacks might have been lulled into a false sense of security by their previous visit to the northwest in 1967 when they had something of a walkover in Manchester. Little did they know that the seeds of our success at Workington in November 1972 were sown five years previously. John Burgess had played in that 1967 game and had been prompted into meticulously planning their downfall the next time they ran across his path. When I arrived to link up with the squad the mood was tremendous and my own spirits rose when I met up and roomed with my old pal Fran who, though still at Loughborough, had been given the task of leading the side. It was a tremendous honour and his success in that encounter should have earmarked him as a great international captain of the future. But more about that later.

Ellis Sports Ground, Workington, proved an ideal venue for the game. The town had been taken over and there was the inevitable full house. When we arrived the crowd was already baying for a colonial scalp and the general atmosphere was fantastic. New Zealand hearts must have sunk when they swept through the beautiful Lake District and suddenly alighted in the Cumbrian industrial town where the steam from the steel works was drifting over the rows of terraced houses. I wouldn't dream of being disrespectful, but Workington was a far cry from the twee Home Counties or the rolling plains of my native Cheshire.

Our line-up that day is one I'll never forget. The side was: Barry O'Driscoll; Tony Richards, Chris Wardlow, Dave Roughley, Stuart Maxwell; Dick Cowman, myself; Frank Anderson, John Lansbury, Fran Cotton, Richard Trickey, Mike Leadbetter, Dave Robinson, Peter Dixon and Tony Neary. It was a nice blend of youth and experience, although the total number of international caps in the side didn't amount to too many. Significantly, three of us went on to break English cap records in our positions – Tony Neary, Fran and myself.

The All Blacks side was: Trevor Morris; George Scudder, Duncan Hales, Mark Sayers, Grant Batty; Bob Burgess, Lin Colling; Graham Whiting, Tane Norton, Kent Lambert, Andy Haden, Ian Eliason, Ian Kirkpatrick, Alan Sutherland and Bevan Holmes. Just for good measure, Sid Going came on as a replacement. There were some people afterwards who claimed we hadn't beaten a particularly strong side, but I for one don't go along with that. You don't get bad All Black sides.

The build-up to the game was incredible and it was my first experience of a Burgess team talk, although I had heard the Lancashire lads speaking of Burgess as though he were the Messiah. We had all had a glass of sherry to calm our stomachs and the glasses were on a table in the room. Burge stripped off his shirt before he even started his talk. There he was in a string vest, kneeling on the floor at the side of the table with his eyes bulging and the veins in his neck pumping blood at a dangerous rate. He looked just like a samurai and the

41

words came flooding out. At one stage he brought his fist down so hard on the table as he pressed home a point that he smashed five sherry glasses into little pieces.

Burge and I have had our differences of opinion over the years but I have to hold my hands up and say that was an absolutely fantastic team talk. He told us how the north had been humiliated by the All Blacks on the last two occasions they had met and how the pride of the region had to be restored that day. He used all his usual ploys, of course. There were telegrams from little old dears living in the backstreets of Barrow and in the backwoods of Fleetwood and newspaper clippings bandied around the room. The cuttings said we were going to be swamped. The whole thing was a brilliant brainwashing exercise by John. He had even compiled a book on the opposition called 'Black Bastards', in which he had analysed their strengths and weaknesses. He had waited and worked for years for that day and when we finally took the field we were ready to take on the world, with a distinctly glazed look in our eyes. There was no way we were even going to consider the All Blacks as unbeatable and that was reflected in the way we went about the task of beating them.

Trevor Morris put New Zealand ahead with a penalty, but Chris Wardlow hit back with a dropped goal. Even when Grant Batty crossed for a try we hammered back at them and put in Stu Maxwell, the Cheshire wing, for the first of his brace.

No matter what they attempted we had an answer worked out to deal with it and one of our best ploys was in using Wardlow at fly half in defensive lineout situations instead of Dick Cowman. That left me with the task of doing any necessary kicking if we won the ball but the plan was devised to stop the All Blacks peel. It worked like a dream too because Chris was a real handful for a back. On one occasion an All Black forward came powering round the back of the lineout only to be met with the full force of Chris who smacked him back several yards.

Chris also had a slight hand in the try that clinched the victory for us. A long throw to the back of a lineout just inside the New Zealand half was palmed down beautifully by Tony Neary to Fran who burst through the midfield with Dick Cowman in close support. When Fran was held, Dick took the move on and flung out a pass to Chris who, instead of attempting to catch, put the New Zealand defence on the wrong footing by simply flicking the ball on and into the path of a grateful Maxwell who took it on the full to streak past on the outside.

The crowd went wild, sensing that a historic victory was on the cards. By that stage Going was on the field, Colling having gone off injured. Even then Burgess, whose adrenalin must have been doing remarkable things to him by that stage, was thinking quickly because Going ran straight on as Colling was helped off. Burge ran to the touchline to protest that Colling's injury hadn't been checked by a doctor and Going had to retire over the touchline to spend a frustrating two minutes waiting to be given the go-ahead.

Not even Sid could have changed the run of the game at that late stage. We were leading 16–14 and there was no way we were going to surrender that advantage, however slight. They threw everything at us in desperation, but the crowd were still baying at them. Steam was still pouring over the rooftops, it had started to hail, and they were two points down with only five minutes to go. I remember thinking to myself that those New Zealanders were an awful long way from home.

When the final whistle sounded the stadium simply erupted. There were bodies everywhere, slapping backs, trying to shake hands. Fran was carried from the field – no mean feat in itself – and the most difficult task of the afternoon seemed to be getting back to the safety of the dressing room. I marked the day down as the greatest in my life until then.

Of course, Burge gave another team talk – this time to the press and anyone else who wanted to listen – and the

All Blacks were left to ponder over their second defeat of
the tour, which also happened to be the first English
provincial win against a New Zealand touring side. They
weren't in much of a mood for watching it again on
television because when we tried to take in the recorded
highlights in the hotel lounge later that night, Keith
Murdoch switched off. He was destined to figure prominently later and was actually sent home for an incident in
Wales. At Workington, however, he incurred the wrath
of Chris Wardlow and there was something of a fracas
before peace was restored and we relived our memorable
afternoon again. It must have been quite a surprise to
tough-guy Murdoch. He can't have had too many
centres squaring up to him during his career, but that
was Chris!

I got a good press the following day and that did my
cause no harm at all. Within two weeks I had partnered
Alan Old in a North side that walloped the South and
South West 31–9 in a divisional game at Broughton
Park. There seemed to be nothing I could do wrong at
that stage in my career and people were tipping me for
an England place in the not too distant future.

When the England selectors announced the team to
play New Zealand at Twickenham, I was selected as a
replacement along with Dick Cowman, Dave Roughley
and Peter Dixon, who had all played at Workington. Jan
Webster was at scrum half with Alan Old as his partner.
The All Blacks managed to salvage some pride with a 9–
0 win.

I stayed on the bench for the next match, against
Wales at Cardiff and surprisingly found myself back
there the following week when the Barbarians played the
All Blacks in the final game of the tour.

I had gone down to Sale for a training session when I
got a message to travel to Cardiff. That led to another
fast exit from base and when I set off by train the
following day I still believed I was actually playing in the
game. However, Jan had cried off and I was taking over
on the replacements' bench.

It was probably the most memorable Barbarians game of all time. It turned into a fifth Test because the Barbarians selected Lions who had returned victorious from New Zealand with Doug Smith and Carwyn James.

My career up to that stage had been full of surprises and discoveries but it was an unbelievable experience to mix with the likes of Gareth Edwards, Mike Gibson, J. P. R. Williams, John Dawes and Willie John McBride. Gareth Edwards was extremely nice to me and I found him to be a typical scrum half, a chirpy sort of fellow and an extrovert. I had never been in such exalted company before and I was puffing the old chest out a little when the lads named two penalty moves after me. When we worked out in training they decided to adopt two moves used in short penalty situations at Loughborough and which the North used as recently as their 1983 meeting with the All Blacks at Gateshead. To differentiate between the two moves they became known by the Barbarians as Steve One and Steve Two.

There was an unusual happening that weekend. Unusual because coaching of the Barbarians has always been regarded as taboo. It happened on the Friday afternoon when we were all called together to a room at the hotel. None of us knew why we had been summoned and as we stood around waiting for something to happen John Dawes told us he had brought someone along who wasn't supposed to be there and who had been smuggled up the hotel fire escape. Then, the door opened and in walked Carwyn James. I had never seen the guy before but the '71 Lions responded straight away by falling silent whilst Carwyn gave a fantastic team talk. It was a very quiet talk, a total contrast with John Burgess's table-thumping style.

Barry John, who had been the lynchpin of the side in New Zealand, had retired, so Carwyn focused nearly all his attention on Phil Bennett. He had seen Phil work the old magic playing for Llanelli but he hadn't seen him quite repeat that form at international level. Carwyn told him, with everyone hanging on his every word, that he could dance and he could sidestep. The All Blacks, he said, couldn't play against that style of play so Phil had to play it that way the next day.

'You must do it from anywhere you want on the field. You must do it. You must express yourself,' he told him. Then he went on to talk about other things with the rest of the side. To this day I am convinced that the magical try the Barbarians scored the following afternoon, and which is still shown on television as the greatest try ever, was due to Carwyn. I am sure that had he never gone to that room and told Phil what to do, Phil would have rifled the ball into touch. Instead, he fielded the ball in his own 25 and produced three magnificent sidesteps to launch the move that Gareth finished off in the corner.

I had roomed with a young lad called Tommy David, who had been brought into the side at the last minute, and he finished up one of the heroes. I also succeeded in having my first brush with the Barbarians committee. Barbarian jerseys are treasured items and they are always handed back after a game. I think the committee would burn them rather than give them away, but after that marvellous performance they relented a little and said the players could keep them.

Later I was approached by a Ba-Bas official who said, 'You haven't played for the Ba-Bas, have you?'

When I said I hadn't actually been on the field he said, 'Well, if you were a gentleman you would give your shirt back.'

My riposte was, 'That's OK then because I don't qualify.'

I kept the shirt and the guy was really upset. He said Gerald Davies and Mervyn Davies had both cried off the game and even they hadn't got a Barbarians shirt.

Well, I had mine and two weeks later I was to add to my collection.

4

Into the Minefield (1973)

After England had been taken apart by Wales at Cardiff Arms Park the week before the Barbarians game in January 1973, it was likely that the selectors would follow the customary pattern and make changes for the next game, which was against Ireland in Dublin.

In fairness to Jan Webster, who had played against Wales, I considered him to be one of the few players to come through that contest on the credit side. He certainly hadn't played badly – not that he ever did – but I was very much the golden boy at that time and it seemed as though everybody – especially the press – wanted me in the side. And, no matter what anybody else might think, I happen to believe the press can have some influence on selection, or at least those rugby writers whose opinion the selectors respect.

When the selectors gathered to select the side to play Ireland, other factors were at play than just form. The previous season neither Scotland nor Wales had travelled to Lansdowne Road to play their scheduled games because the IRA had issued death threats to players. Similar threats were made to members of the English camp and, whilst the RFU was determined to fulfil the fixture, they didn't want any player to feel he had to make the trip. Naturally, wives, parents and girlfriends were probably more concerned than the players and the RFU were right in giving individuals the opportunity to pull out of the game without jeopardizing their chances of selection in the future.

Sam Doble and Peter Larter decided they wouldn't

make the trip but the rest of the squad said they were prepared to travel. I was quoted in the press as saying I was prepared to go to Ireland to play in a minefield if necessary ... and I meant it. First I had to be selected, however, and I thought Jan had done enough to retain his place in the side.

When the team was announced I was giving a lesson in the college gymnasium. Ken Ingman, the England Schools cricket selector who had persuaded me to apply for the job at the college, came in to tell me I was in the side. In view of Jan's performance I was very surprised, but it was a nice feeling when I rang my parents to tell them I was about to win my first international cap. They must have had mixed feelings about it in view of the venue but I couldn't wait to get there. Tempered with that elation though was a genuine feeling of sympathy for the man I replaced. I was a great fan of Jan – especially after watching his fantastic performance against the Springboks the previous summer – and I apologized to him the next time we met.

I trained very hard that week and prepared to take a rain check the week before the international in keeping with tradition for players about to make their debut. But, irony of ironies, Sale were drawn away to Wilmslow in the John Player Cup that day. As I had taken a fair amount of stick from certain people over my decision to leave Wilmslow for Sale the previous summer, I was determined to play in the cup game. I did. And we won.

The following Thursday I travelled down to London and we trained at the Stoop Memorial Ground before leaving for Ireland the following day. It was a pretty unreal situation because of the IRA threats and security was very tight. There was a police escort from the airport to the Shelbourne Hotel and that effectively became our prison for about forty-eight hours. We were very highly protected and weren't allowed out of the hotel.

That aspect didn't worry me too much because I am rather partial to hotels. I have no set pattern on match days but like to lie in bed watching television and reading the morning papers. I don't eat before a game normally but like a conveyor belt providing me with coffee on the hour. Some players get up early, eat a hearty breakfast and go for a stroll, but that's not for me. In my early days with Wilmslow I was amazed when I travelled with Cheshire and they took us out for lunch before a match.

As there was usually steak on the menu, and as I was a poor student, it seemed too good to miss. I got into the habit of asking a waitress to wrap mine uncooked in a piece of tinfoil. Then I would pop it into my blazer pocket and take it back to Loughborough where I would enjoy the rare luxury of a steak dinner.

I spent the morning of my international debut quietly but I wasn't nervous. I have never suffered from nerves. Instead I get excited.

One of the pleasantest tasks on debut day is opening all the telegrams. A mass of them were delivered to the hotel or were waiting in the dressing room at the ground and that was when it was first brought home to me how much these games mean to other people. There were messages from Jim Greenwood and other friends from Loughborough, from Cheshire county, Sale and Wilmslow, and from clubs I had never been involved with but which simply wanted to wish me all the best. My old school, King's, Macclesfield, remembered me and, of course, there was a telegram from my mother that read: 'Have a belter.'

Over the years I had grown fond of Fran Cotton's parents and they hadn't forgotten me either. Like their famous son, they are great patriots and Lancastrians. Their message to me that day was: 'Congratulations. Have a great game. Give 'em some stick and plenty of northwest fire.'

We had the police escort again for the short journey to the Lansdowne Road ground and I started to pick up some of the marvellous atmosphere of Dublin during international weekends. The atmosphere in the dressing room was sparked with anticipation but John Pullin, our

49

skipper that day, was the ideal man for my first international. He was a good captain, very sensible and level-headed, and it was his style to keep things quiet and low key.

I went into the privacy of the toilet to pull on the white jersey and I kissed the rose because it meant so much to me. All the way through school I had wanted to play for England. I had got close at both cricket and rugby but thought I would never achieve my great ambition. It was a magical yet emotional moment to realize I had finally made it. To play for England was everything because I have always been fiercely patriotic, regardless of which sport was involved. If the England cricketers lost a Test match or the soccer players had lost an international game I wouldn't speak to anyone, just as when, in my younger days, Manchester United had come unstuck.

I see nothing wrong in taking sport so seriously. Indeed, I believe that it is terribly important to feel that way; it is a good guide to watch top international players and see how they react to defeat. Fierce patriotism can even compensate for such things as having slightly less ability than other players. There are some people who claim that sheer natural ability marks the difference between a great player and a good player but I believe an equally important ingredient is competitiveness. The greatest geniuses I have ever seen on a rugby field are Gareth Edwards and Gerald Davies and both were pretty competitive. In my book defeat has to hurt and, no matter what sort of façade you achieve, it has to chew you up inside. During my years with England the truly great players were forwards like Fran Cotton and Tony Neary, who were both highly competitive. Those who haven't seen him at close quarters might find it hard to believe but Nero even had the edge on Fran when it came to competitiveness.

However competitive I felt that afternoon, I was still in for something of a shock when I ran onto the field. To win your first cap is a rather special moment anyway, but the circumstances of that afternoon ensured it would be indelibly etched on my memory. We were hit by a wave of noise as the Irish crowd, so obviously grateful that we had ignored the threats, gave us a five-minute standing ovation. I was told later that the Irish players who were set to follow us onto the pitch had to be held back until the noise died down.

It was a very emotional experience and we were all terribly proud to be there. But, in one respect, it was eerie because we were all looking around apprehensively for any glint of sunshine on steel in the crowd. To be honest, we didn't know whether to stay close together when they played the national anthems or scatter to make ourselves more difficult targets!

That unforgettable Irish welcome lasted only until the first whistle of the afternoon, I'm afraid. There might be some who suggest that the unreal atmosphere probably affected our game – the warmth of the welcome weakening our resolve. It wasn't a case of that, however. We were quite simply beaten by a better side on the day. There was no way we could match them for experience and, significantly, that was the international in which both Willie John McBride and Mike Gibson won their fortieth caps for Ireland. By comparison, our most capped player was John Pullin, who had a mere twenty-seven to his credit. There were four new caps, two on either side. Roger Uttley made his debut for England in the second row and flanker Jim Buckley and centre Dick Milliken won their first caps for Ireland. In addition to McBride and Gibson, the home side also included such great names as Tom Kiernan, Fergus Slattery, Ken Kennedy, Sean Lynch and Ray McLoughlin, with John Moloney and Barry McGann as the halfback pair.

You never experience anything quite like your debut game, no matter how long you play rugby. The speed of everything and the level of commitment take you by surprise. Suddenly the game you have been playing for years has just gone up ten gears and the eighty minutes are over in a flash. You end up leaving the field unsure as to how well or badly you have played. Even so, I felt confident that I had done myself justice, even though we had lost the game 18–9. Our one real bright spot came when Tony Neary broke through for a try during one of the few spells when we managed to produce sustained pressure.

Satisfaction with my own performance seemed to be justified by comments afterwards and one newspaper article referred to it as being a 'dream debut'. That was not for me to say and my main consideration, once I had got over the initial disappointment of the defeat, was to soak up the atmosphere of an international weekend. An atmosphere, I might add, that is not quite the same if you haven't actually been out there where the action is.

With that first international firmly beneath my belt I was ready to continue my, thus far, unhindered progress and that was ensured when the selectors gave me their vote of confidence for the next match. That was against the French at Twickenham and, although they had only managed to beat the Scots by a narrow margin, they were on the crest of a wave. By contrast we had suffered two defeats, admittedly away from home, and France were being tipped to beat us at Twickenham.

My opponent in that game was Max Barrau and the scrum half was considered a real danger man, having been largely responsible for the destruction of the All Blacks earlier in the season. A glance at their line-up was sufficient to have many people going along with the theory that France were favourites to win the game. They had Walter Spanghero as captain and his front five included René Benesis, Jean Iracabal, Alain Estève and Jean-Pierre Bastiat. Behind the scrum, Barrau had Jean-Pierre Romeu as his partner and the threequarter line comprised Roland Bertranne, Claude Dourthe, Jean Trillo and Jean-Pierre Lux.

Surprise, surprise, after ten successive defeats in Europe we ended up outplaying the French to a far greater extent than the 14–6 scoreline suggested. Our forwards raised themselves to the task to such an extent that they overshadowed their illustrious opposite numbers and my task was eased a little when Barrau went off injured. He was replaced by the less effective Richard Astre, of Béziers.

David Duckham scored two tries, the first created for him by Peter Preece, whom I rate as one of the most talented English backs I have ever played with or against. It was a great loss to the game when he brought his playing career to a very premature close but I suspect he had become disenchanted with the game and the frequent strange decisions made by selectors. Peter was a very skilful player and possessed tremendous pace, which he displayed to good effect whilst playing sevens later in the season.

After the victory over the French I was being hailed as the English Gareth Edwards and a great deal was being made of my long spin pass, which I'd learned from watching Chris Laidlaw. While still at school I was also shown how Rugby League scrum halves used the same passing technique, staying on their feet – and therefore still in the game – at the same time.

When I first started playing the game at school the big thing was the sharp dive pass, but the spin pass eventually took over and the longer your pass, the better player you were thought to be. Yet, like the pendulum of a clock, the emphasis has swung back to the short, sharp pass favoured by players like Dave Loveridge and Nigel Melville.

Anyway, I had a long spin pass, tended to be rather physical and as a consequence was being talked about as a second Gareth Edwards. It was with that enviable reputation that I returned to Twickenham to play against Scotland. For the second successive game the forwards produced the goods and we took Scotland apart. As with the French, the victory margin of 20–13 was ridiculously small considering the amount of possession we won. Peter Dixon collected a brace of tries and Peter Squires and Geoff Evans also crossed Scotland's line. The press were kind to me once more and my playing career seemed to be maintaining its upward momentum.

That wound up the Five Nations' Championship for the season with all five countries finishing level on 4 points each – making England champions and wooden spoonists at the same time.

My next objective was to ensure a place in the England party due to tour Argentina that summer but, before that, I was involved in a very pleasant international weekend. Scotland decided to bring their centenary season to a close by staging a World Sevens competition. That was right up my street because I had been involved in sevens since my schooldays. The thought of playing that particular brand of rugby at such a high level had tremendous appeal, especially in a country with such a strong sevens tradition.

During my time at King's School I had played in a very successful sevens side which one year took on and beat the best school outfits in the country. That side included my old pal Steve Midgelow and Andy Sokill, whose path I crossed again years later when he was covering rugby for the *Daily Express* and the *Daily Star*. Loughborough also took the sevens game seriously and Sale had a pretty useful line-up when end-of-season tournaments came round.

Quite apart from the rugby it was a marvellous weekend in Edinburgh. Although things were highly competitive on the field, the occasion had a strong social bias as some of the world's top players were gathered together and all stayed at the North British Hotel in the city. Some of those players, from New Zealand, South Africa and Australia, were already in Scotland to play in special centenary fifteen-a-side games and stayed on to represent their countries in the sevens tournament.

Not everyone had played sevens before and it was great fun watching Don Rutherford trying to coach the French players in the game's very different tactics. The All Blacks were also new to the game but, being All Blacks, they caught on pretty quickly and very nearly reached the final.

The eight competing countries played in two groups of four and we had an easy first outing against the French whose natural flamboyance can be a hindrance when playing sevens. We won 22–0 and our only setback was an injury to Dave Duckham, who took no further part in the event. He was regarded as something of the trump card in our pack but Peter Rossborough came into the side in his place and he helped us see off a Scottish President's Seven 26–16 to bring us to our final group game against Wales.

One look at the Welsh side would have been enough to scare most people off, but, like everyone else but the English, they made a crucial error in selection. And I always thought that was a largely English disease! Their pack comprised J. P. R. Wiliams, Mervyn Davies and John Taylor – two back-row forwards and a fullback – whilst Gareth Edwards was at scrum half with Phil Bennett as his partner. Gerald Davies played in the centre with J. J. Williams outside him on the wing. Despite the array of talent, we had an easy 24–10 victory and that was due entirely to the fact that we had the only hooker and prop in the competition.

Our pack was Fran Cotton, John Gray and Andy Ripley and that trio simply prevented the Welsh from getting the ball. Without which, of course, there is no way you can play sevens successfully! I was at scrum half, Peter Rossborough came in at fly half, Peter Preece was in the centre and Keith Fielding – unquestionably the fastest thing on two legs in the entire competition – was on the wing. In terms of pace, our three technicians in the pack were all capable of doing a little bit in the loose too. Fran was no slouch despite his size, Andy was a talented track runner and John was a tremendous all-round athlete ... something he demonstrated when overhauling flying Frenchmen.

Keith showed his pace against Wales when I chipped a ball over the top for him. Although he was being chased by Gerald and J.J. he still found time to stop in his tracks, pick up the ball and then accelerate away from them again with remarkable ease. That was genuine pace and Peter Preece proved himself to be only marginally slower.

We finished our group game against Wales and then, because the final was going out live on television, we had only five minutes' rest before taking on Ireland. It was asking rather a lot of us because we were absolutely shattered, especially Keith, who had produced several long sprints and didn't look capable of taking the field again. There was just time for a quick rub down whilst gulping half a cup of tea before heading back into the fray against an Irish side that had surprised everyone, probably themselves as well, by winning the group we had all expected the Scots to win at a canter. Scotland were the sevens kings in most people's eyes but the selectors made the mistake of overlooking Duncan Patterson. He had made Gala tick for years and was the play-maker, as I discovered on my sevens excursions into the Borders.

Ireland, who included Fergus Slattery, Mike Gibson and Willie McMaster, were a good deal fresher than we were and stormed into a quite commanding lead. Poor old Keith seemed too knackered to run in the tries. He looked finished and I had to keep moving the ball left to Rippers who ran in a couple of great tries whilst Peter Preece managed a third. We were still trailing at the death and that's when Slats burst through, flinging a pass inside. I managed to intercept it almost on our own line and immediately fed a long ball out to Keith who succeeded in summoning up all his remaining energy for one last effort. He raced the length of the field for a try under the posts – his ninth of the tournament – and John Gray converted to give us a 22–18 victory.

The celebrations went on late into the night and, providing the Scots never arrange another tournament, I suppose I will remain a reigning champion at something!

5

Setback (1973)

The aspect of rugby I had taken to most readily was touring and I could hardly have hoped for a more exotic baptism. England had been planning a visit to Argentina during the summer of 1973 but politics played a hand and a tour to New Zealand was arranged instead with a stop off at Fiji en route. So, having been introduced to one paradise, I was heading for another, an experience I wouldn't have missed for the world.

By that stage I had started to get my size nines beneath the England table, so to speak, and was feeling quite at home with my team-mates. Fran and Nero were also in the touring party, along with characters such as Andy Ripley and Mickey Burton who both became popular travelling companions.

It didn't take me long to fall in love both with the Fijians and their beautiful island and I had an early insight into their attitude to rugby. We were taken to watch a game between two teams representing the east and west sides of the island and that contest was like something I had never seen before. It was pouring with rain, none of the players wore boots and the touch judges had leaves for flags. After about half an hour a player was injured and, despite treatment from one of the touch judges, had to be carried off, at which point the touch judge got into his kit and took his place on the field. In addition to carrying the flag, he doubled up as sponge-man and replacement. The match was played with tremendous spirit and was great fun.

The rain tumbled out of the sky again when we had a

training session but I arrived late because I had been receiving physiotherapy treatment in the dressing room. When I splashed my way on to the quagmire where the lads were working out Stack Stevens ran up and pushed something down my back that was cold, slimy and wriggled. I was convinced it was a snake and literally ripped off my shirt to release it while the rest of the players were convulsed with laughter. I was horrified to discover that my very temporary lodger was a frog that must have been a foot long.

Apparently the rain had attracted hundreds of huge frogs and the lads had been having valuable sidestepping practice trying to avoid them as they splashed around the paddy field of a pitch. I've never been so frightened in my life and that wasn't the end of my biological experiences on that tour. Later, when we were in New Zealand, I was asleep in the hotel when I suddenly realized, to my horror, that something cold and slimy was crawling over my body. I didn't know what the hell it was and grabbed for the light switch before punching and kicking the 'thing' around the room. The lads, as ever, were peering at me through the window and laughing their socks off. My nocturnal visitor was a fish they had caught earlier in the day but one that was not destined to finish up on a plate covered in batter and surrounded by chips. That little fish ended up down the lavatory!

We only played one game in Fiji, at Suva, a major occasion for the islanders who created the sort of atmosphere I was never likely to see anywhere else in the world. England fielded a strong side and it was just as well because we only just managed to beat the Fijians 13–12. It was a very hard game which was made even more difficult by a somewhat one-eyed referee, and it was only in the dying minutes that Peter Squires scrambled clear to score the winning try. The experience, in Suva's steamy heat, had been rather akin to playing a hard squash match in a sauna.

The Fijians were super, sociable people and I developed a very healthy respect for their way of life and the way they play their rugby. Both are full of fun and the rugby has flair and excitement. Although forward technique – or the lack of it – leaves them struggling over here, they can be an extremely difficult side to beat on their own mango patch, as the Lions discovered in 1977 on their way home from the New Zealand mudbath.

With that enjoyable experience out of the way, we were on to the really serious business of the tour. Landing in New Zealand was like entering a different world. It was rather like arriving in our Lake District on a bad day.

We settled into New Plymouth to play our first game against Tarakani and, as I had played in Suva, Jan Webster was drafted in at scrum half. It turned out to be a hard game which we lost 6–3, our only points coming from a penalty by Peter Rossborough.

The next port of call was Wellington where my pal Fran was honoured with the captaincy for the game and Roger Uttley was brought in for his first international appearance as a number 8. It was a fantastic game, but I kept getting caught at the back of the scrum and, being somewhat naïve in those days, couldn't figure out what was going wrong. I discovered later that the fault lay with Roger, who admitted that he hadn't quite known what he was supposed to be doing. What made things worse was that Fran kept popping his head out of scrums and demanding to know 'What the bloody hell's going on back there?' Roger and I eventually got the business sorted out and after the interval we fought back really well. Unfortunately not well enough to prevent ourselves being on the wrong end of a 25–16 scoreline. What I hadn't realized, until he told me a few years ago, was that I had been playing against a promising young flanker called Graham Mourie. Andy Leslie also played that day and he had quite a hand in affairs. My view that we had done well to claw our way back from a 21–3 deficit at half time was not one shared by everybody.

The next game was against Canterbury in Christ-

59

church and we again finished up on the wrong end of a
19–12 scoreline. Jan was at scrum half and Peter Squires
managed a brace of tries, but Peter Rossborough and
Alan Old somehow contrived to miss nine kicks at goal
that would have given us a comfortable victory.

There was a week's break before the solitary Test
match against New Zealand and, although I didn't know
it, I was heading for my first major setback since
establishing myself in the first team at Loughborough.
Sandy Sanders, who managed the tour, called me up to
his room and, after asking how I felt things were going,
suggested that I looked unfit. I told him I thought I had
played two good games and had managed to sort out the
difficulties encountered early in the Wellington match.
He gave me a thorough going-over and although he gave
no direct indication that my place was in jeopardy, I
realized I could be on the way out.

When they announced the Test team at the training
camp, and Jan was in instead of me, I was mortified.
John Elders was coach and I really laid into him while
refusing even to speak to Sandy. I was very upset and
threw the bricks out of the pram. John asked if I was
normally a slow starter and I replied that I thought I had
established my level of fitness by being able to make the
blindside break that led to Peter Squires's winning try in
Fiji.

But I had no animosity towards Jan. I had roomed
with him and we had talked about the decision to drop
me and he had been sympathetic. We had struck up a
great relationship and I had enormous respect for him as
a person and as a footballer. He would never let any side
down and played in a way that was ideal for the game in
Auckland. In my book he took the man-of-the-match
award, even though it was extremely frustrating to have
to sit in the stand and watch him.

Came the day of the Test and the history books show
what happened. England had been written off by the
pundits and, for once, New Zealand's selectors blew it.
They were so convinced they were going to walk all over

us that they picked a back line to run the ball and then put Sid Going at scrum half. They were keen to emulate the 1971 British Lions but picked the wrong personnel as Going was being asked to play a game that was unnatural to him. The selectors also picked a new fullback, R. Lendrum, just as South Africa had done the previous year, and Jan put him to the sword.

On the day our pack was tremendous. Chris Ralston cleaned out the highly rated Peter Whiting, the back row of John Watkins, Andy Ripley and Tony Neary blotted out Going, and Jan was given the freedom to launch his aerial invasion. We won 16–10 with tries by Tony Neary, Peter Squires and Stack Stevens and we were treated, late in the game, to a moment I'm never likely to forget. That was Fran selling two outrageous dummies before executing a beautiful chip to the corner for Rippers to race through to touch down. For reasons unknown to me the referee disallowed the try and blew for time, leaving poor old Rippers lying on the ball.

Watching a marvellous victory from the stand when you are desperate to be out there, a vital part of it, isn't the greatest of experiences. I spent the afternoon sitting alongside Mickey Burton, who wasn't the happiest man in the world either because he had lost his place to Fran, who had returned from injury. Fran was quite a size even in those days, and when we left London he had hopped onto the scales at Heathrow Airport. The needle shot up to 19 stones and poor Fran went white with shock. What he didn't know was that Mickey was standing behind him with his foot on the scales.

I soon realized that our West Country boy was quite a character and we enjoyed a few cracks together on the tour. We teamed up for the last week after being dropped and kidded ourselves we had gone on strike. It became our practice to slip out for a few quiet beers away from the rest of the lads and we had a lucky escape one night when we wandered back into the hotel at 2 a.m. and walked slap bang into two of the press guys. Fortunately they were very good about it and didn't report our nocturnal habits to the management.

Mike is absolutely marvellous value on tour and I think all tours need someone with his humour and outlook on life. He has the ability to lift players out of depression and to put down the worst of the heavies who often attach themselves to touring parties. He would reel off yarns and his store of humour never seemed to run dry, which is one reason he became such a sought-after after-dinner speaker when he retired from the game. Had he wanted, he could have become a professional comedian.

As a rugby player, he was one of a new breed that had started to come into the game. Mike was the opposite of those who had entered the game from more traditional sources. No public school or grammar school for him. He had to fight his way up. In a way I think that helped him because it turned him into a hard man and a tough competitor blessed with what you could probably best describe as street cunning. It took a player of Fran's ability to get him out of the England side and the sad thing is that he should have won many more caps than he did, preferably playing as Fran's partner.

Another great character, although one I had discovered earlier, was Andy Ripley. In those days he had long hair, wore John Lennon spectacles and was what you might describe as bohemian. I took him home a few times and he developed quite a liking for my mother's cow pie and was introduced to Boddington's bitter, which delighted his palate to such an extent he reckoned Boddies was better than drugs!

He is another who should have played for England more often and there was a lot of excellent raw material for a first-rate coach to work on. He was a tremendous athlete and his all-round ability has been clearly demonstrated by his success in 'Superstars'.

Before we left for New Zealand he didn't bother to turn up for the kit measurement session, with the result that his tour blazer was miles too big for him and hung off his tall frame like a tent. One day he actually swopped it in the street for a total stranger's jacket. A very surprised Australian set off for home resplendent in an England R F U blazer and Rippers strolled along with the rest of us proudly sporting his secondhand lumber jacket. When we clambered aboard the team coach, Sandy Sanders started beating his stick and demanding to know what Andy had done with his blazer. He nearly went bananas when he found out and Andy was promptly ordered off the coach until he had reversed the transaction. Miraculously, Rippers eventually found the chap in a shopping centre and persuaded him to part with the item that would have made him the envy of his friends.

Apart from my disappointment of being left out of the Test side, I enjoyed the tour. John Pullin was an ideal captain, greatly respected by the lads, as he had been in South Africa the previous year. He was a quiet man, did things his own way and never tried to be anything other than what he was. At no stage did he put himself up as the big tactician. His attitude was quite simple and is summed up by his comment, 'We'll get the ball and you lot sort it out behind.'

When I got back to England and into the cricket scene again I had to think seriously about my rugby future. It had never occurred to me that I could lose my international place because everything until then had gone perfectly smoothly. I had been moving very steadily and very surely up the ladder and, on arrival at the top, had felt I would become a fixture for a time. As I concentrated more on hitting the small red leather ball out of the park I knew that in rugby terms I had a real fight on my hands. I wasn't upset about Jan replacing me but I felt the selectors wanted a particular style of play to be adopted against New Zealand. I was prepared to change my style of game to suit requirements but neither Sandy nor John Elders explained to me the type of game they wanted us to play Down Under.

The next season saw me back in an England shirt, albeit with the number 23 beneath the rose. The game was against Japan and I was very impressed by their ability, agility and the speed at which they accomplished things. My partner in that England Under-23 side was Neil Bennett and there were one or two interesting names in the line-up. One of my touring companions, Peter Squires, was on the wing and the fullback was a great character who spared my blushes on the same ground seven years later, Dusty Hare. Mike Rafter was at blindside and Phil Blakeway was at prop.

I still thought I had blown it so far as the senior international scene was concerned, especially after the way Jan had played in the New Zealand Test. Incredibly, the selectors dropped him and brought me back for the game against Australia, who toured Britain during the autumn of 1973. Jan was as bewildered as I was at the decision. But, as the years rolled by, it became a very familiar pattern of selection for the pair of us.

The North played the Australians during the week of the international at Twickenham so I wasn't able to play in their encounter at Gosforth. Malcolm Young, the talented Gosforth scrum half, got his chance in that match and he was to get his England chance later when I was totally out of favour with the selectors.

The Twickenham game brought me face to face with the highly respected Australian scrum half, John Hipwell, who led his country that day. He was clearly a great player but he struggled that afternoon because his pack was well beaten. Their cause wasn't helped much either when winger Jeff McLean missed five straight penalties and Russell Fairfax only succeeded with one from four attempts.

Nero, Rippers and Alan Old scored tries for England and we won 20–3 to complete a remarkable achievement. In the space of fourteen months we had beaten every side in the southern hemisphere.

Odd, isn't it, that we were champions of the southern hemisphere yet poised to embark on the Five Nations' Championship trail that would leave us clutching the all too familiar wooden spoon.

64

6

The Yo-Yo Years (1974–79)

The inconsistency of England team selection, so painfully brought home to Jan Webster and myself, left me unsure as to just what the selectors were looking for from a scrum half. But I decided the one thing I could be certain about was that there was no room for complacency – especially after playing on a winning side!

My season was destined to be plagued by injury, but I didn't know that as 1974 dawned. I launched into the New Year in high spirits brought on for reasons that were more than just traditional. While most people were working off the ravages of Christmas and preparing for the physical challenges of New Year's Eve, the England selectors, in their infinite wisdom, pitched us into a full-blown trial in the shape of an inter-divisional game between the Midlands and North at Nottingham. It was a crucial game for me because I was opposing Jan, who was partnered by my old team-mate, Alan Cowman, whilst I had Alan Old for company. The game was affected by a strong wind and, although the North turned round 12–4 adrift at half time, the writing was on the wall. In the second half the floodgates opened, sweeping us to a resounding and very satisfying 53–12 victory. That served as another warning that the North was a veritable hot bed of rugby talent and my only regret is that it was largely ignored by successive national selectors.

On a personal note, however, it seemed that success might no longer be a handicap because I was chosen to play against Scotland at Murrayfield. That's when fate played its hand and for the first time in my career I suffered a bad injury. The week before the international I played for Sale against Bristol and pulled a hamstring. It was with very great reluctance that I withdrew from the international and Jan stepped into my shoes again, only to find the residence a very temporary one because England lost 16–14. My mates Fran and Nero performed a try-scoring double act but Andy Irvine proved the thorn in the side of the rose for the umpteenth time by landing his traditional match-winning penalty.

That game was England's first step down the road towards the wooden spoon and I regained fitness in time to get involved in the second downward step against Ireland at Twickenham. It was one of those ridiculously high-scoring games which Ireland won 26–21 and in which the old maestro, Mike Gibson, ran in a couple of tries. I got through the game all right but, in retrospect, I think I probably returned too soon after my injury, although the selectors must have been satisfied because I held my place for the next game against France in Paris.

Having lost our two opening games, the match was a fairly daunting prospect but our spirits rose when we arrived in Paris to be greeted by a blizzard. As the Parisian traffic skidded and bumped into each other rather more than usual, we slept contentedly in our beds, dreaming of getting to grips with fifteen frozen Frenchmen. Needless to say, that little reverie didn't last long because we awoke to warm sunshine and clear blue skies.

The change in the weather seemed to make the French crowd noisier than ever. The brass bands were playing, the horns were blowing, peas were in good form in the whistles and fireworks had you thinking you were surrounded by artillery. The infernal racket became so intense that it was impossible to hear what was being said five yards away. Even our lineout signals had to be switched from verbal to visual, but the cacophony of sound didn't stop us from playing better than we dared hope. At one stage we were trailing, but pulled back a 9-point deficit to draw 12–12, thanks largely to a great try scored by Dave Duckham.

My joy at staving off another defeat was short-lived. That was the weekend of the Paris air disaster and at our hotel on the Friday evening I had stayed up playing cards with an old friend, John Cooper, the Loughborough athlete who was working as a representative for Adidas. Sadly, he was one of those who died in the crash.

Although we weren't aware of it at the time – on the day after an international in Paris you are not really aware of very much at all – the England players had very nearly been passengers on that plane. Apparently, the original plan had been for the players to travel separately from the officials but we ended up flying back together.

When we heard about the disaster I was worried about my parents because I knew they had been in Paris for the match. As I drove back from London I kept stopping to telephone home but my fears turned out to be unfounded because they had changed their plans and driven to France instead of flying there. It was during the drive home that I heard on the radio that John had died in the crash. It came as a terrible shock and I had to stop the car while the news sank in. I found it very difficult to comprehend that less than forty-eight hours earlier we had been laughing and joking together and reminiscing over our college days.

Injury prevented me from playing in the final championship match against Wales. That put paid to any lingering hope that I might just clinch a place on that summer's British Lions tour to South Africa. Earlier in the season people had been talking about the possibility of my going on tour as deputy to Gareth Edwards. Our similar styles probably helped that speculation but Ireland's John Moloney had had a good season in helping Ireland to the title. Bloody hamstrings. They have been the bane of my life!

Jan was brought back for the Welsh match at Twickenham and I settled down to watch the game on television at home. We actually beat the Welsh for a change and whilst I was pleased for England's sake I was pretty cheesed off from a personal point of view. Jan, as always, played really well and when an extra game was arranged against France to raise money for the dependants of those who died in the air disaster, he was in the side and I was back on the replacements' bench.

So, the Lions went off to South Africa. I would have given my right arm to have been part of that historic tour. It was not to be, however, and I eased the pain by making my first visit to America with the Anti-Assassins. More of that elsewhere!

The 1974–75 season I was quickly back into an England jersey, playing for an Under-23 side that swamped Tonga 40–4. Dusty Hare was in the team along with another travelling companion, Peter Squires, and two lads from St Luke's College, Exeter, whom I got to know rather well later – Mike Rafter and Mike Slemen. What I didn't do was play for the North against the Tongans. That distinction went to Lancashire scrum half, Brian Ashton, who was starting to push through towards the England side. It was perhaps significant that Lancashire's John Burgess had taken over as the national coach.

That was the time when my weight troubles started. I had thoroughly enjoyed myself in America and my social life at home left little to be desired. I was living in a house, known locally as Cirrhosis Nook, with four pals from Loughborough College – Steve Midgelow, Garth Ormond, Steve Rule and Gordon Graham. The place was also something of a clearing house with people passing through; at one time we were joined by a couple of lads who had left their wives. Perhaps we should have become marriage guidance counsellors because our lifestyle eventually drove them back to their wives!

In addition Sale was a great social club and there was always plenty going on. There was no organized coaching. From time to time people made the odd comment about my weight but they were never the right people and the comments weren't made in a constructive way. That was the time when I needed someone in authority to tell me that I was a stone overweight and to get rid of it. But it never happened and life was there ... to be lived.

By now Burge was established as the great white hope for English rugby. Oddly enough, his contribution a couple of years earlier, when he was cast aside, would have been a good deal more constructive. When he coached England in Japan people criticized him for being too basic in his approach, but what he had been trying to do was get the underlying structure right before attempting to widen the scope. Players simply weren't capable of doing routine drills properly and he had wanted to instil that discipline into them.

When England turned to him again, instead of grabbing the opportunity to prove his methods, he went completely to the other extreme. He produced a string of short penalty and back moves that just weren't on and the whole thing became too complicated. That was a great pity because I believe the methods he had applied with Lancashire and the North West would have been very effective.

Sadly, several talented players never figured at that time and one of those cast from the squad was Chris Ralston, whom I rated as the best lineout jumper on the scene. I met him at a dinner some time later and he told me, in that delightfully far-back drawl of his, 'If you see that baahstahd Burgess, tell him that in my day second-row forwards were supposed to jump, not take short penalties.'

Andy Ripley was another to go under the new regime and I thought that was a mistake too. He had so much to offer in addition to his athleticism and his strengths were never utilized. The plan seemed to be to mould players into a pattern rather than moulding a pattern around players and their varying abilities.

Bill Beaumont got his big break that season, although I think it came a shade too early and he would probably agree with me on that score. At the same time things didn't look too good for me because I knew Burge was a Jan fan and didn't hold me in the highest regard. I don't know why, but we tended to clash; it could have had something to do with the fact that we are both pretty extrovert characters.

Anyway, whatever the reason, I ended up on the bench for the opening game in the championship against Ireland in Dublin, having played for the Rest in the trial. Jan and Pete Rossborough got involved in a bit of a cock-up near our own line and we lost the game by 3 points, but there seemed no reason to make changes because it's never easy winning in Dublin. The selectors did react, however, and the axe was swung once more, this time falling on the neck of poor old Alan Old.

They brought in Martin Cooper for the French game, I was still on the bench and we were annihilated even though the scoreline of 27–20 in favour of France looked reasonably respectable. That defeat produced the old backs-to-the-wall situation and I felt terribly sorry for Fran, who had been made captain that season and deserved better. He must have had a sense of foreboding as we trailed down to Cardiff to face a powerful Welsh side and it wasn't exactly the surprise of the century when we were given another good hiding. The one bright spot for me was being given the chance to play against Gareth Edwards for the first time when Jan was carried off and I went on as replacement. John Pullin had also been injured during the game and that meant my pal Wheelbrace – Peter Wheeler – got on the field as well.

It's never easy going on as a replacement at the best of times but I reckon the toughest situation is going on at the Arms Park when your side is getting well and truly stuffed. Me being me, I started chattering at the lads as soon as I got on to the park and at the first scrum beseeched them to 'Get stuck into these bastards.'

Gareth wasn't having any of that and told me that if I wasn't careful I would get my features rearranged. I responded that if they were he wouldn't be the one to do it. Believe me, I was really psyched up and managed to get in a couple of good tackles because I was determined not to let Gareth make a break. At the final whistle I was quite pleased with myself because, although we lost the game 20–4, we drew the second half and Gareth didn't make one break, although he kicked superbly.

With Jan injured and me having played well – or so I thought, because Burge and the chairman of selectors, Alec Lewis, told me so – I reckoned I had an excellent chance of making the side to play Scotland in the final game. With such a prospect before me, I really recaptured my enthusiasm and put in a lot of hard work in training the following week. I even imposed total abstinence on myself. But when the side was announced not only was my name missing, I wasn't even on the bench. Jacko Page had been drafted in and Brian Ashton was chosen to keep a seat warm in the stand. What really upset me was the knowledge that I had always been able to get the better of Brian, even when he was playing in a powerful Lancashire side and I was struggling along with Cheshire. In fact, he used to joke that I must have put a jinx on him.

It was the biggest setback in my entire career and marked the time when I lost both patience and confidence. Until then I had assumed I stood a good chance of touring Australia with England in the summer of 1975 but now that prospect went straight out of the window.

The only sympathy I felt at that stage, except for myself, was for Fran. He was injured for the Scottish match, which England managed to win to save a few blushes, and the captaincy was handed to Tony Neary. I suspected that injury played right into Burge's hands because I had the feeling all along that he really wanted Nero as captain. Nero had captained Lancashire even though Fran was in the side. I have always had enormous respect for Nero, have admired him as a truly great player and have enjoyed a close friendship with him over the years. But he was always something of a loner, very much his own man, and I think he was less suited to the role of captain than Fran was given the right opportunity. Fran could have become the complete captain. He was a master of his front-row trade, had the

71

ability to motivate players and was tactically aware.
Francis was no great big thick prop, but he just might as
well have been that season. Unfortunately, Burge never
gave him the opportunity to develop in the way that Bill
Beaumont was later allowed to do. Burge was far too
dominant a character. He took the training sessions, he
took the team talks and Fran had very little say in
anything.

England went off to Australia and I joined a sort of
rejects' tour to Zimbabwe (or Rhodesia as it was then)
which turned out to be a rather better venture. Burge
and Alec Lewis went Down Under with a bunch of kids
and paid an alarmingly heavy price for the lack of
forethought. Things went wrong from the start, with
both Fran and Nero getting injured and five replacements being flown out before the tour was over. Luck ran
out on Brian Ashton when his wife was taken ill and he
had to fly home before he could make his challenge for an
England cap. I was pretty sure they would send for me to
replace him, but one of the Irish lads I was touring with
had us scratching our heads when he announced that he
had heard England had called up a fellow called Rum. I
thought he must have been drinking it, but it later
transpired that the player was Yorkshire's Ian Orum.

Needless to say, I was pretty upset about that, and
John Watkins, who had been told categorically that he
was first reserve, was even more angry when he discovered that Peter Dixon had been called up ahead of
him. That just about summed up the shambles. What
with Mickey Burton getting sent off and the side losing
both Tests, it was reasonable to assume that English
rugby was at an all-time low. We had even lost our
reputation for winning abroad. The tour was supposed to
prepare us for the championship ... the one ten years
hence!

One consequence was that all three scrum halves –
Brian, Ian Orum and Peter Kingston – succeeded in
playing themselves out of contention for the following
season. Whispers were heard along the grapevine that I

stood a good chance of getting my old slot back if I got myself fit, so I trained particularly hard during the remainder of the summer and had a good county season with Cheshire. We even beat Lancashire that year but lost the play-off against them when Fran accidentally demonstrated the efficiency of a bacon slicer by cutting my leg open. By the time seventeen stitches had been inserted and I had returned to the fray, it was too late.

Things were going well on the club scene too that season with Sale having a good run in the John Player Cup, including an excellent victory over a strong London Welsh side. The big worry in that game was doing something England had never been able to achieve, namely keeping J. P. R. Williams quiet. We managed it too by clever use of Steve Rule, a tough-tackling fly half who is now playing Rugby League. As the London Welsh fly half wasn't very physical, we suspected that if he was put under pressure he would ship the ball, which meant J.P.R. would be brought into the line. We told Steve to forget the fly half and loop round to take the Welsh fullback every time he came pounding through with the ball. To a lad destined to play the professional code to a high standard, halting big men in their tracks was all part of an afternoon's work.

Although they were beaten on the day, the London Welsh lads still managed to enjoy themselves. They drank with us all evening and returned to the clubhouse the following day for some of my mother's famous cow pie. By the time they left there wasn't a drop of drink left in the place, literally. Not only had all the beer been consumed, every bottle of spirits had been emptied as well. We even ran out of lemonade.

Sale finally went out at the semifinal stage when we came up against Gosforth, who were overwhelming everybody with their juggernaut pack. We lost Fran, who was sent off for responding by flattening Malcolm Young. Even with only fourteen players on the field we succeeded in giving the Geordies a run for their money, but their powerhouse pack won the day.

73

That season, 1975–76, England picked a side to play against the regions and I was back in favour. Peter Colston had taken over as coach and when we played against the South and South West at Kingsholm I was paired with Martin Cooper. Before the game Peter Colston took me on one side and told me he wanted me to do nothing other than keep passing the ball out to Martin. That, I thought, was a piece of cake and I proceeded to follow his instructions to the letter. My previous experiences should have prepared me for the next shock, but didn't, and I was staggered when the final trial teams were announced. I had been relegated to the Rest and a lad who seemed to have sprung up from nowhere, Headingley's Mike Lampkowski, had leap-frogged into the England scrum-half berth.

My partner in the trial was Alan Old, with Coops playing outside the new boy. We all soon realized that England selectors were as surprising as ever because what they seemed to have overlooked completely was the fact that Mike couldn't pass accurately. Poor old Coops was picking up minesweepers all afternoon as the lad's passes were flying all over the place, but something must have impressed the selectors because they promptly picked him to play against Australia, who were touring over here to let England get their own back.

I was back on the bench for the Australia game and, as often happens, young Mike had a very impressive debut. There was no denying that he was very strong and he succeeded in getting over for a try, although the Aussies were not what you would term 'hot' opposition. The venom they had displayed back home was absent in the mother country.

Mike got the vote again, this time for the visit of Wales, and England were absolutely terrible. There was a mix-up behind a scrum (not to be recommended with Gareth around) and Wales scored en route to another comfortable victory. The travelling circus then moved on to Murrayfield where we stuffed Scotland out of sight yet still managed to lose. Mike made a couple of searing

74

breaks in that game but then proceeded to overdo it so that it became counterproductive, and Alan Old was on the sort of service fly halves have nightmares about. Then followed a disastrous game against Ireland, which we lost by a solitary point. By that stage I was feeling genuinely sorry for Mike. In a few games he had been totally destroyed and neither the coach, nor the selectors, had done anything to help him by improving his service. We had the silly arrangement at squad sessions of Mike working with the forwards whilst I practised moves with the backs. They should have had me popping the ball into the scrums with Mike spending his time passing out to the backs.

What followed can only be described as a total fiasco. I was recalled to play against France and Martin Cooper was chosen as my partner, with Alan Old on the bench. When we met up in London before flying to Paris, Peter Wheeler, who wasn't fully fit anyway, found that he had left his passport at home and had to chase off to collect it. Coops had had an injury and was subjected to a rather bizarre fitness test. For half an hour they made him tackle Fran, Andy Ripley and Roger Uttley, just to make sure that if he wasn't unfit when he started then he would be by the time he finished. Miraculously he came through the ordeal without a problem and was promptly declared unfit. We could only deduce that the selectors didn't want him in the side in the first place.

The obvious assumption then was that Oldie would step up, but we were puzzled by the arrival of a strange guy who wandered around in playing kit. It transpired that he was Chris Williams, who played for the RAF, and he was introduced to me as my halfback partner for the game. As I started training with him, Alan Old marched up to Alec Lewis and all hell broke out. The pair of them were going at it hammer and tongs in the middle of the training pitch while the rest of us conducted an unopposed session all around them. It had to be the most farcical situation ever.

We were at sixes and sevens before we even took the

field. I remember Fran telephoning Twickenham for tickets the day before the team was announced and asking Don Rutherford who would be at number 8. When he was told it was Gary Adey, from Leicester, he couldn't believe it. Gary was a very good footballer, but we were hoping for a really big man like Andy Ripley because we needed someone around 6 feet 6 inches tall to cope with Jean-Pierre Bastiat. When Fran asked how they expected Gary to compete against Bastiat he was told that Gary was an international player. Well, so was Jan Webster, but you wouldn't have asked him to mark a giant Frenchman.

Wheelbrace finally showed up in Paris, but wasn't allowed to play, and John Elliott was flown out on the morning of the match to sit on the replacements' bench.

It really wasn't any great surprise when the French took us apart limb by limb. Their front row that day was heavyweight boxer Gérard Cholley, Alain Paco and Robert Paparemborde; the engine room was Jean-François Imbernon and Michel Palmie; and the back-row trio was Jean-Claude Skrela, Jean-Pierre Bastiat and Jean-Pierre Rives. What took place during the eighty minutes following the first whistle is best forgotten. The French pack was one of the best of all time and we simply weren't up to the task.

I was involved in one mix-up with Gary that led to one of the French tries in the 30–9 defeat, but that wasn't a factor in the end. We were outgunned by a great front row, a second row of pure scrum tractors and Bastiat who wandered up and down the lineout winning ball at will. It was as easy as walking round an orchard picking apples off the trees. The only thing that saved us from total disaster was the appalling form of the French backs. They missed four early try-scoring chances and after that the big French forwards merely shrugged and stopped giving them the ball. Their tactics from that point were effective, to say the least. Bastiat would win the ball, become enveloped in blue shirts and the blue wave would then trundle relentlessly downfield.

We knew enough French to have gathered from their conversation amongst themselves that the ball wouldn't be moved out to the backs, but that information was of little assistance to us. At one stage four of the French forwards burst from a maul, driving right through the heart of our pack and bearing down on me. I was steamrollered out of the way and they all fell over our line. They scored four tries in that fashion, two of them being credited to Paparemborde.

Afterwards we were completely shellshocked and couldn't even match them in the singing stakes. It is always traditional at the dinner after the French game in Paris for both sides to sing and our choirmaster was always Fran. But on that occasion when we looked at Fran after the victors had performed their party piece, he just looked back at us and said, 'I'm not man enough to sing with them.' The defeat, and the manner of it, had hurt the big feller deeply.

It was the only time I could recall playing behind an England pack that had been annihilated. Of course, it then turned into the night of the long knives and I found myself involved in a row with John Reed, of the *Sunday Express*, who had made comments in his column that I took exception to. Normally I wouldn't have had a go at the press, but the game, the crazy selections and daft observations in print finally got through to me. I don't always agree with what they write, but I know they have a job to do and have never held anything against them when they criticized me. But I have wondered at times just how many of the influential writers really know what they are talking about.

The writer I have always enjoyed reading is John Reason of the *Sunday Telegraph*. At least he gets it right 95 per cent of the time, goes to the heart of issues and doesn't try to dress things up. I suppose you could almost call me a Reason fanatic because he is the man I most like to read and I have also always found him to be an interesting man to talk to. Where I would criticize him is when he occasionally has a bit of a down on people and won't let go, as happened with Tony Neary a few years ago.

Early in the 1976–77 season I played for the North and Midlands against Argentina at Leicester and not only did we win well, we also fielded a side that was to have a strong influence on the Grand Slam success a few years later. If only the England selectors had realized that at the time.

I was still carrying a little bit of weight but felt I had probably worked my way back into the England side – an optimism that was to be shattered when Gosforth's Malcolm Young kept me out of the North side. Dejection crept in when he was named opposite Alistair Hignell at an England trial, but I managed to squeeze back into the picture as skipper of the Rest at the final trial at Twickenham. Having picked up a tip from Bastiat, I had Rippers going up and down the lineout, which he did with a similar success ratio to the Frenchman. By half time we were ahead but that was the point when the selectors appeared on the pitch to deprive us of both our second rows. Our lineout signals went with them, but I left the field satisfied that I had given my best final trial performance.

The press seemed to think so too because they were tipping me, but when the team to play Scotland in the first match was announced I was on the bench and Malcolm was in the driving seat. It was becoming soul-destroying because every time I felt I had got myself back in line the selectors would produce someone else. In fairness to Malcolm, I must say that he was a good player and I suppose that with such a strong Gosforth connection in the side at that time his selection made sense.

England beat Scotland and Ireland, lost narrowly to France and were finally beaten by Wales. I was on the bench for every game and got on for a spell in the French match when Malcolm was injured. The following year, 1977–78, I didn't even get a trial. I think they would have picked my mum before me and I reached the conclusion that my international career was over. It had had its moments of magic but many, many more moments of utter frustration.

Having made up my mind that I was out for good – I hadn't been picked for the squad for two years – I was surprised to find that not only did I not miss it, I had no real desire to get back. That was due to my total disillusionment with the England set-up and, to be honest, the planning and preparation at national level in those days was absolutely pathetic. In a sense attending Loughborough had been a disadvantage. Having been coached properly there and then moving to the higher echelons of the game, it was disconcerting to find everything done on a very amateur basis.

I often found selectors to be completely out of touch and coaches who were nice guys but who really didn't have a track record to speak of. John Elders fell into that category and I always felt a little sorry for Don White, the first person to coach me at international level. Don was a smashing chap and had been a great player in his time, but he was a victim of England's headlong rush into coaching simply because the Welsh were coaching successfully. One of Don's sessions I attended at Coventry involved mainly physical jerks and I later watched flabbergasted as Jacko Page dive-passed when practising short penalty moves without being told not to put himself out of the game in that way. I suppose John Burgess was the first England coach to have the right coaching background. Even Mike Davis didn't have a coaching track record in the senior game.

So far as selection is concerned, you only need to be on the international circuit for two seasons to discover who the best players are and it is very frustrating when the selectors don't pick the best players available. Things have improved to some extent now but it wasn't terribly nice playing for England during the seventies. We were continually being beaten, people were always taking the mickey out of us and after most games you just wanted to disappear. Maybe the whole thing got to me more than most, but I simply hate losing and I was never a cap gatherer. The mere fact of playing for my country was never enough for me. I wanted to win for England and I reached the stage where I didn't want another cap because defeat hurt too much and I had absolutely no respect for the selectors.

I'm not blaming them completely for my own yo-yo-style playing career and am the first to hold up my hands and say that I was a mite wayward and wild during the seventies. But I desperately needed someone to get hold of me and straighten me out and nobody ever did. They discussed my fitness and my attitudes, but always when I wasn't there; today, if I saw someone like Nigel Melville put on a stone in weight, I would call him and talk to him about it. Young players need people to show that sort of concern.

In my own case, England didn't really have a scrum half with my ability once Jan Webster left the scene, so somebody should have been finding out why I was wasting my talents. People might well turn round and say that was my responsibility, but I think those involved at the highest level of rugby should do whatever is necessary to produce a successful side. Rather than tell me to lose weight, they chose to ignore me and in the meantime tried just about everything else under the sun at scrum half without finding an answer to their problem.

Selectors also made a mistake of labelling me as a bit of a joker, a lad who didn't really take the game seriously. Whatever they thought, I believe I was a good deal more competitive than most on the park. I enjoy a laugh and a joke as well as the next player, even on the field, but it doesn't signify you are treating a serious game as a lark just because you have a smile on your face. One of the nicest sights in recent times was Paul Simpson, the Bath forward, laughing his way through England's victory over New Zealand in 1983. He had a marvellous game, full of good, honest endeavour and commitment, and even though the All Blacks presented him with a scar to remember, they couldn't wipe the grin from his face.

What successive selectors have failed to realize is that they are handling a bunch of young men who have an awful lot on their minds. They are usually pursuing a new career, pursuing girls, pursuing success on the rugby field. They may be filled with doubts, find the pressure hard to take or may become too big for their boots. Every player is different and that's why they need fatherly advice from time to time and to be told exactly what is expected of them, both on and off the field.

I'm not suggesting selectors should live in the players' pockets, but there should be greater contact between them. England have usually achieved good results on tour when the selection process is reduced to just the manager, coach and captain. Our overseas results probably proved the point that we always had the players but failed to select them in the right combinations at home. It seemed such a criminal waste of talent.

When I thought my own international career was over I was depressed to think that so many great players had been mismanaged. One of the most glaring mistakes was the failure to field Fran Cotton, Peter Wheeler and Mickey Burton as England's regular front row. That could have developed into one of the greatest front rows in the history of the game, yet they only played as a unit on a couple of occasions.

It was obvious to most people during the seventies that we needed a proper graduation system for both coaches and selectors. Just like players, they needed to start from a club base and work their way up the ladder by proving themselves at county and divisional level before getting anywhere near a national post.

As a coach, Mike Davis finally turned up trumps, but even that had an element of luck about it because the selectors really had the Grand Slam team of 1980 forced on them by the North's success. I don't think Budge Rogers and Co. were necessarily better selectors than those we had before but they did introduce a degree of consistency for a time. They slowed the topsy-turvy selection process although I always felt that some of us would be moved out quickly enough if half a chance presented itself.

What I grew to like about Mike Davis was the way he learned from people around him during his first season as national coach and that helped him later when he really came into his own.

I don't think we should have a coaching supremo, as happens in soccer; rather, the coach should also be the chairman of selectors. If I were appointed England coach I would have a rough idea of the side I would want to put out. And in selection I would want people on my side of the table who thought about the game the same way that I do. People like Fran Cotton, Bill Beaumont, Peter Wheeler and Tony Neary. People make selection complicated, whereas it should be a very simple process in that you pick the best side available regardless of whether a player is eighteen or thirty-eight – having first determined the style of game you want to play so that you would know the styles and skills you are looking for.

People say that at the end of the day it's down to the players out on the field. To a certain extent that is true, but it helps enormously if the selectors have ensured the right fifteen are actually out there. As a youngster you dream of playing for your country. You regard it as the greatest thing that could possibly happen to you, but once you get up there you realize the quality of that experience depends on five selectors. And if you don't particularly respect them, your idea of playing for England can be suddenly devalued, as it was for a large number of us during the seventies.

During one season, 1975–76, which I spent on the replacements' bench in practically every game, one of the replacements had to go on to play out of position, only to be dropped from the squad immediately afterwards. Barrie Corless had to go on at fullback, Peter Preece on the wing and Neil Bennett in the centre. At least Peter Wheeler and I felt fairly secure for once because we were only covering our normal positions!

The lads used to make up games such as the 'Golden Guillotine', in which they staggered round the dressing room pretending to clutch gaping wounds at the back of their necks. That players should start mocking the reckless axe-wielding selection process says something about the way things were done during that period. I found that relationships, such as they were, between selectors and players tended to be rather false. Most selectors would talk about anything except the game, unless they had had a drink or two and then some of them could get quite poisonous.

When they finally dispensed with my services in 1977 I settled comfortably into club rugby at Sale and, away from the constant pressures of a yo-yo international career, I simply became happier and happier and chubbier and chubbier.

7

Passport to the World

The pressure of playing at the highest level of a game as physically and mentally demanding as Rugby Union would probably become intolerable for an amateur if it weren't for compensations that, for me at least, have made the hard work and sacrifice worthwhile. There is obvious compensation in being considered good enough to represent your country and in achieving success at both an individual and team level. But there are added compensations in the friendships you establish and the pleasure you derive from meeting great personalities from other sports and other forms of entertainment. And, let us not forget the compensation of being handed a passport and airline ticket to the world.

If ever you hear anyone suggest that Steve Smith is a good tourist, you can take it from me that they know what they are talking about. I enjoy nothing better than flying off with a bunch of great blokes, meeting new people, seeing new places, playing a little rugby and having a little fun. During the last decade I have travelled the globe in pursuit of both rugby and fun and the riotous trips are stored away in the memory almost as fondly as recollections of major sporting achievements. Quiet, serious people often get homesick when they are away for any length of time but touring suits my personality perfectly. And that must show itself because people keep inviting me back!

My favourite tropical paradise, where I am usually to be found during the Easter holiday, is Bermuda. It is only a small island but, so far as I am concerned, it is a paradise on earth. Everywhere is beautifully green, the roads are very narrow with a speed limit of 30 m.p.h., which slows down the pace of life to the right level, and the place is surrounded by a blue-green ocean and white beaches.

The occasion for my visits to Bermuda has very strong Irish connections, almost an essential ingredient if you want a tour to remember. There is a very active Irish community on the island and Tommy Kiernan went across one year to coach the Bermudan Irish side which plays an annual match against the Bermuda island team. A couple of Irish internationals were injected into Tom's side and the opposition followed suit. This practice grew until both sides were fielding six or seven imported international players, the game growing in importance at the same time.

Preparation for the contest begins the moment you step from the plane. Your extremely hospitable hosts introduce you to 'dark and stormers', a rather pleasant drink concocted with dark rum and ginger beer. And that, I can assure you from considerable first-hand knowledge, is a real, bona fide knockout drop, which is probably the last thing you want after a long flight during which the intention has been to see what sort of dent could be made in the airline's liquour supply.

After a few dark and stormers you are handed over ('poured' might be a better description) to your hosts whose task it is to look after you for the four or five days you are on the island. There is a delightful story about former England wing, Peter Squires. He dropped his luggage at his host's house and called back to collect it, and introduce himself to his hosts, five days later when he was on his way back home.

One of the Irish lads didn't even manage to leave his bags. His welcoming party, complete with the obligatory dark and stormers, was a great success. Then he leaped into a taxi and told the driver roughly the district he thought his host's house was in – not having been there before. When they reached the district in question he told the driver he wouldn't be able to miss the house as the lads had told him it was the one with the white roof. What he didn't know was that every house on the island has a white lined roof to collect rainwater, which is then stored in tanks as it's the only source of water on the island. Surrounded by white roofs, Paddy spent the night in the taxi.

I never have any trouble finding my billet. Every time I have been to Bermuda I have been the guest of a fabulous couple, John and Kathy Williams, who have a beautiful house that has the ocean for a back garden. They have a charming daughter and I feel as though I have grown up with the family.

The stories I could write about Easter in Bermuda would fill a book all by themselves and I have yet to meet a player who hasn't had a whale of a time. Mind you, I met a coloured American winger who will be keeping a wary eye out for the dark and stormers. He was a nice lad and incredibly fast but he was one of a rare breed in rugby circles in that he was teetotal. Not once in his life had alcohol passed his lips. Well, we got him on the dark and stormers and it is such a pleasant drink he didn't realize it contained alcohol. By the time he had had ten of them he didn't know whether it was Wednesday or Wembley. In addition to the dark and stormers, our hosts always provide us with mopeds to ride around the island on. Until my dying day I'll never forget the sight of this lad roaring off into the night and all we could see were two big white eyes in the darkness.

When we saw him the following day he wasn't black any more. He had turned grey. Apparently he had got himself hopelessly lost hurtling around and, peering into the blackness ahead of him, he suddenly saw the ocean. He leaped from the machine which shot straight over a cliff into the sea and he was left clinging to tufts of grass for about half an hour, too terrified to move.

Those mopeds were a licence for the lads to maim themselves. I remember leaving one party at which we had each consumed the equivalent of about a bottle of rum and setting off on our machines. I could just make out the lower half of Johnny Horton's face as he peered out of a crash helmet that was miles too big for him. Johnny Murphy, from Ireland, and John Carleton were with us, and as we set off down the street I noticed that the road surface was very greasy following a shower. I could sense there was going to be some fun so I kept about twenty yards behind the others. J.C. was the first to lose control. Incredibly he fell over, hit the ground and bounced back up again in one movement. As I watched with my mouth open he did it again, skinning his shoulder, but still going off in pursuit of the other two. Then Johnny Horton accidentally hit the brake and his moped started spinning around in the road like a top. Johnny Murphy went straight up his backside, shooting over him like a human cannonball and J.C. ploughed into the pair of them. It was like a scene from a Monty Python sketch.

The first three days are always like that but we do try to do a little training the day before the big game. As this is a serious match played in a high temperature you have to perform well no matter how rough you happen to be feeling. You owe it to your hosts, and they expect a good performance. If they don't get one they are unlikely to issue a return invitation, so it's one of those occasions when, for eighty minutes, you have to slip in a cassette and get on with it.

One of the funniest sights I have ever seen there was Tony Neary, who by then had retired from the game. When the invitation was issued he went through the motions of a little light training to prepare himself. He had put on a bit of weight and they played him at number 8, but when the game started it was just like turning the clock back a few years. For twenty minutes he was literally everywhere, smacking people over and playing with the sort of determination one might reserve for a British Lions Test. But gradually one sock slid down around his ankles, a shirt flap worked its way out, then the other sock was rolled down and, most unusual, his hair was terribly dishevelled. In the second half he was frothing at the mouth and as we walked off the field he vowed he would never, ever, play rugby again.

The Irish lads take the game very seriously and whilst we tend to wear any old kit we can lay our hands on, they run out looking immaculate in the green of Ireland with a shamrock sewn on the breast. One of their ever presents is Stuart McKinney, and Hugo McNeill and Donal Spring are popular draftees into the Irish side. After they had been overlooked for the 1983 British Lions tour to New Zealand, and were naturally feeling a bit down, I took Peter Wheeler and John Scott over to Bermuda and they thoroughly enjoyed themselves. Huw Davies also joined us on that trip and as we lay on the beach, toasting ourselves beneath a cloudless sky, I reminded them that life could be a lot worse.

Bob Hesford is another who fell in love with the island and Peter Squires was known to sit by his telephone as Easter approached each year. The year after the punch-up with Wales, during our Grand Slam run, Jeff Squire went out with us. I wasn't sure how things would work out because he had captained Wales that day and some of us had blamed him for firing up the Welsh lads at Twickenham. But things couldn't have gone better and we became great mates.

After Bermuda, my favourite touring countries are America and Canada. It was in America that I first came into contact with women's rugby at a tournament in Washington. I was in a public park, where our games were being played, with Gary Adey, the Leicester back-row forward, when we were approached by a six-foot blonde. She was a really good-looking girl, clad in only a tee-shirt and shorts.

She said, 'Hey, are you guys part of the football team?'

I said we were and Gary just stood there, mouth wide open, drinking in this lovely Amazon. She looked him up and down and said, 'Gee, you must be a forward.'

Gary still didn't say anything so she started to ask me how we packed down in the second row, explaining that

that was her position in a women's rugby team.

I told her how we would get down behind the prop, shove our hand between his legs and grab hold of the top of his shorts. Without a moment's hesitation she dived down behind Gary, shoved her hand between his legs and hung on, saying, 'Yeh, I see what you mean. You can get a really good shove on here.'

By that time, Gary's eyeballs had crossed and steam was coming out of his ears.

We thought it was a joke, but as we started chatting it turned out that she did play second row in a women's rugby team. They were apparently playing their own tournament at the other side of the park, so we went across to watch and were amazed to find all these girls knocking seven bells out of each other. In many respects it was just like a men's team with little, fat, dumpy props, tall second rows and pretty little wingers flying up and down the flank.

The lads wouldn't believe us when we told them about it. So they got quite a shock when the women's final was put on just ahead of ours. They were so transfixed I'm surprised they managed to get through our game later. Naturally, we all got together in the park afterwards and the girls asked us to sing a song for them. We came up with a few melodies but they protested that they wanted to hear rugby songs from England. We were somewhat put out because it was a public park with people walking past pushing prams but tried to oblige by delivering a good standby such as 'Four and twenty virgins. . .' They interrupted us, told us we were singing rubbish and proceeded to reel off some of the dirtiest songs I have ever heard in my life!

There was no clubhouse and no shower block so we were taken to a farm which had a pond and told to use that. The lads decided to pull a stunt on my Sale team-mate, Garth Ormond. He had stripped off and was swimming around the pond with one of the female rugby players when the gang spotted their clothes and decided to burn them. By the time the happy couple strolled hand in hand from the pond their clothes had been reduced to ashes.

The rugby girls also play a tournament in Bermuda and when girls in Britain suggest we lads are lucky to be travelling the world and enjoying ourselves I always tell them they could do just the same as the American girls. They play tournaments all over the place and take the game very seriously. I was chatting to one of them in Bermuda and she asked if I was married. When I said I wasn't she asked if I had a regular girlfriend. I said no and was just starting to ponder where the line of questioning might be leading us when she said, 'Yeh, I know this life, training three nights a week, playing tournaments every weekend, you just can't get a regular scene going, can you?' She was being deadly serious. It was the male situation in reverse.

Arriving in New York for the first time is quite an experience and when I went there with the Anti-Assassins the coach driver, who drove us from the airport to Manhattan, turned on the loudspeaker and told us, 'Here you are boys. This is New York and we call it the Big Apple. Whatever it is you are into ... it's out there somewhere.' Well, I don't know what Richard Breakey, the Gosforth player, was into but he succeeded in unloading his entire tour spending money in one night. He hit New York all right and he hit it big!

We had a great session in the bar that served as a clubhouse and then we each went off with our host. I reckon I drew a lucky straw because my host had the job of looking after six air hostesses. Well, I'm a helpful sort of bloke and that was my introduction to New York. The following day we all met back at the bar to go for a training session and bodies were dragging themselves in like rats from the streets of New York. Goodness knows where they had all been or what they had been up to, but nobody was sober enough to be suffering from jet-lag. Lads were trying valiantly to force down orange juice before the training session, but Des Seabrook, who was our player–coach, had a feel for the situation. He took one look at the apparitions in front of him, ordered beer all round and cancelled the session.

That was a great tour but the old constitution took something of a battering. When you stay in hotels, as you do on international tours, it's possible to crash out occasionally in your room. But, on a hosted tour you move from one set of hosts to the next and while you become progressively knackered they are always fresh and raring to give you a good time. When we weren't socializing or playing we were in transit, and on the North American continent that can be a very time-consuming process. Coach journeys were usually a minimum of six hours and one train journey was in excess of twenty hours. We travelled through the Rockies from Vancouver to Calgary and, although the scenery was breathtakingly spectacular, the players couldn't sit gazing at it for that length of time. Once boredom set in we got down to the task of drinking the train completely dry. Then, when we arrived at Calgary, we were whisked off in a coach and driven to a brewery. As we struggled with half pints of beer our hosts were clearly disappointed and kept making remarks to the effect that they had been led to believe we guys could drink. They obviously felt they had been grossly misled.

That was the tour on which three of the lads actually looked like drinks. Steve Gustard from Gosforth, Steve Christopherson of Waterloo and Nick Spaven from Sale bought themselves complete Budweiser outfits. They had Budweiser hats, tee-shirts, shorts and socks and walked around in that ridiculous garb calling themselves the Bud Men. They looked absolutely crazy.

Just before leaving for home, Steve Gustard slipped a few packets of sugar into Steve Christopherson's case. When we landed at Manchester Airport he raced ahead to tell the customs men what he had done and asked them to stop the lad dressed like a can of Budweiser. The customs men played along beautifully and when Steve Christopherson passed through they asked to look into his case. Steve was laughing and joking with the rest of us until they found the little packets of sugar. They ripped one open, dipped in a damp finger, tasted the contents and looked knowingly at each other. Poor Steve was still trying to puzzle out where the sugar had come from when the customs officials asked if he knew he was carrying narcotics. As they marched him off to a cubicle he was shouting, 'Tell them I spent all my money. Tell them I didn't have any money for drugs.' They stripped him, even shone a torch up his backside and ordered him not to leave the country. When he finally came out he had turned a whiter shade of pale.

Gosforth lads like Steve Gustard were good company to tour with and when I went back to America with Gosforth to play in the bicentennial competition in Boston there were five British sides travelling out on the same plane. It was a pretty chaotic flight. That was also the first time I got to know big Maurice Colclough. Clutching a bottle of Drambuie, he sought me out, promptly filled a tumbler with the stuff, drained it and then said, 'I believe you can drink a bit. Have one of these.' Well, Drambuie and aftershave are all the same to me. I took a raincheck.

On that trip we were joined by former Ireland prop Ray McLoughlin and I remember the call asking him if he was prepared to let his name go forward as manager of the 1977 Lions to New Zealand. He was upset at having to turn the chance down because of his business commitments, which was a pity because I think he would have made a great Lions manager.

The tour of America and Canada with England, when I was captain, was a thoroughly enjoyable experience. One of the things that made it particularly enjoyable was the knowledge that we were technically better than the opposition and could therefore relax rather more than would have been wise on a tour to one of the older rugby-playing countries. Coach Mike Davis threw in the towel after two games; if he could get the lads to bed by 4 a.m. on a match day he was doing well. As for big Maurice, he was only seen during the nocturnal hours.

I would hate anyone to think that, by saying what I have, I am in any way belittling American rugby. I love their cavalier attitude to the game and they have some big men who play the game hard. They also have pace but are rather short on technique and until they acquire that they won't trouble us seriously at that level. The game over there is played for fun and that's why their players enjoy it so much. It is so different from other American sports, which are totally and unbelievably professional.

One of the highlights of the tour was a visit to the home of the famous Dallas Cowboys, where Springbok Naas Botha tried to break into American football. I told the Cowboys coach that the only way they could improve on their players would be to have selective breeding, and that's not quite so far-fetched as it sounds. They already go back three generations in establishing a player's potential in the same way we study horse-racing form. One club put money down on a three-year-old because his pedigree was so good.

The professionalism of American football is so high that if it were applied to rugby over there we could all retire now. The weight-training room at the Cowboys headquarters had numerous machines, each specialized to develop muscles in different parts of the body. We tried out the equipment and then the management allowed the England players to go through a few tests they use on newcomers. We came out of them reasonably well. Clive Woodward was fastest over the shuttles and the coach said he was quite impressed but added that Clive really needed another 20 lb. Woody said that if he put on that much weight he would lose his speed but the coach seemed quite confident he could not merely add the necessary weight to Clive's body but also knock a second off his time as well. He also reckoned Steve Bainbridge had a good build but needed another 3 stone.

In terms of climate and scenery, South Africa and Zimbabwe take an awful lot of beating but, in the case of the former, the apartheid question hangs over the country like a dark cloud. To my mind the fact that they include the word 'apartheid' in their constitution shows naïvety.

In trying to understand South Africa one has to attempt to see things through the eyes of someone born there. I am quite sure a lot of whites are brought up over there to believe that Blacks are second-class citizens and accept the situation as quite normal. If my mother had indoctrinated me at the age of five I would probably have grown up believing it. But I think things are starting to change for the better and the South Africans must realize they can't hope to suppress so many people for ever. I detected a change on my last visit and I am convinced sport and television have played a major role in that.

One has to remember that South Africa has only had television for a few years, so people born and brought up there had little with which to compare their way of doing things. Young people in South Africa are becoming aware that Black and White mix freely in other countries and it is only by people widening their horizons that real change will come. I believe that South Africa will get it together eventually.

Part of the problem derives from the fact that the country is split into different factions; it isn't quite as straightforward an issue as simply Black v. White. The tribes themselves have differences and I have heard it said that in South Africa the Blacks hate the Whites, the Whites hate the Blacks and the Afrikaners hate the lot of them. That, of course, is a gross oversimplification of the problem but the Afrikaners are rather like a race apart. Orange Free State is where you meet the real short-hair brigade. A few of us were invited to the home of one Afrikaner who insisted on playing us the radio commentary of their game against the Lions the previous year. We sat there for an hour and a half listening politely and drinking his beer, but it was all in Afrikaans and we couldn't understand a word.

In recent seasons there have been differing opinions about the level of racial integration in rugby and, so far as I could make out on my last visit, the game is pretty well integrated now. The difficulty in making a proper judgement is that you have to allow for the fact that the Blacks don't particularly like rugby. They are soccer daft and regard it as their game. But there were three coloured lads who played for South Africa in the Five Nations tournament in 1983, including Erroll Tobias. Of course, the first thought that will spring into some minds is that they were only put into the side because the game was a showpiece. I don't buy that one. They were there on merit and nobody could have reached their level without having played a good standard of club rugby for some time.

I've always tried to be fair-minded, ready to hear both sides of an argument, and for that reason I have insisted on being taken into the black ghettoes and townships. (I have also been to some of the camps in Zimbabwe and conditions there are absolutely terrible.) In South Africa it is easy to have the wool pulled over your eyes and that's why I wanted to see the black townships for myself. Their reaction to me was very definitely hostile but you couldn't blame them for that. At one camp all the men were sitting around drinking booze from an old petrol can. They were probably all facing a future devoid of tangible hope. The problem is that there are too many Blacks for available jobs but the hope of work attracts them to the cities where they end up living in appalling corrugated huts.

I found the atmosphere in Zimbabwe a good deal healthier. The first time I visited the country we had a black coach driver; he wouldn't have been allowed on the same bus in South Africa. He was a really nice bloke but the hours he was expected to work were appalling. He would take us somewhere at six in the morning and would still be waiting to drive us home at three the following morning. At the end of our two weeks all the lads chipped in well and when we handed the money over to him he broke down in tears. I don't recall how much it was but it was probably more than he could earn in months.

There was another instance when Peter Wheeler and I used to take on Ned Byrne and Willie Duggan at golf. Whenever we arrived at the course we were besieged by caddies because the English had a reputation for tipping well. We finished up with a regular youngster called Sam and he was magic out on the course. If you sliced your ball into the jungle he would chase after it and by the time you arrived he would not merely have found the ball but polished it and produced the right club for the next shot.

He was so good that one day Willie decided on a little test. On one hole a lake stood between tee and green, and Willie was curious to see what Sam would do if the ball landed in the lake. He promptly chipped his shot slap bang into the middle of the lake and we had to chase after Sam to stop him diving in after it.

When we expressed our gratitude at the end of the first round he was delighted with the tip, but the club professional came to us later and gave the money back to us. He said they would get greedy if they were given too much. Anyway, Sam got his money in the end because we slipped it to him quietly later.

One of the great things about touring is that you get to see things and places many people only read about or see on television. Victoria Falls was one of the most impressive natural wonders I have ever seen, apart from Fran, and watching lions enjoying lunch in the Kruger National Park was also highly entertaining – especially when the warden ventured from the security of our vehicle. He knew from experience just how close he dared approach and stopped at the point where one more step would have meant curtains for him. I stayed right where I was, but later showed a fair turn of speed when one of the lads disturbed a slumbering croc at a crocodile farm we had been taken to. I'm told they can move very quickly on dry land but I wasn't waiting around to put the theory to the test.

I found the South African attitude to rugby very

The first trophy I ever won. That's me sitting second from the right in the front row of the Poynton Primary School football team

My first experience of captaincy with the King's School, Macclesfield, under 15s side

Opening the batting for Brooklands with an old Manchester United favourite, David Herd

Wearing my Sale colours with my old friend Dick Trickey backing up as always

Probably the start of it all. Making a break at Workington when the North West beat the All Blacks 18-16. Providing protection are, *left to right*, Mike Leadbetter, John Lansbury and Fran Cotton

Facing the 'ferocious' tackling of my old mate John Horton. We have been playing for and against each other since the age of twelve

Another score for the North in the 21–9 victory over the All Blacks at Otley with aerial appreciation

The fabulous Lancashire side that won the 1979-80 county championship title. *Back row (left to right)*: Dave Tabern, Roger Creed, Terry Morris, Trevor Simon, Keith Pacey, Colin Fisher. *Middle row*: Des Seabrook (coach), Eric Evans (chairman of selectors), Keith Aitchison, Dave Carfoot, Tony Neary, Laurie Connor, Jim Syddall, Fran Cotton, Eddie Deasey (team secretary), Alan Gott (Lancashire secretary). *Front row*: John Heaton, Peter Phillips, Mike Slemen, Bill Beaumont, Jim Walsh (President), John Carleton, Tony Wright, Peter Williams, myself, Kevin O'Brien

One of my proudest days when the North beat the All Blacks 21–9 at Otley. *Back row (left to right)*: Des Seabrook (coach), Andy Simpson, Tony Neary, Fran Cotton, Jim Syddall, Steve Bainbridge, Roger Uttley, Peter Dixon, Dave Tabern, Steve Tilley, Colin White, Peter Squires, Alan Hosie (referee). *Front row seated*: John Carleton, Kevin O'Brien, Tony Bond, Bill Beaumont, Mike Slemen, Tony Wright. *Kneeling*: Peter Williams, Nigel Melville, Alan Old, myself

Bill Beaumont on one of his famous charges. New Zealand captain Graham Mourie
can only stand and watch

Cheers Fran. The big fellow gets the ball to me despite the attentions of All Black
Andy Dalton

Apart from the guy with the big ears at the end, the whole of the front row in this Grand Slam season picture in 1980 have Lancashire connections. Not to mention four in the back row. The line-up, *back row (left to right)*: Peter Wheeler, Nick Preston (Lancashire born), Roger Uttley (Lancashire born), Nigel Horton, John Scott, Fran Cotton (Lancashire), Tony Neary (Lancashire), Phil Blakeway, John Sargent. *Front row*: John Horton, Mike Slemen, Bill Beaumont, Steve Smith, Tony Bond, John Carleton and Alan (the ears) Old.

Scoring a try against Scotland 1980

Three Sale lads represent England. A great honour for the club — Tony Bond, Fran Cotton and myself

Billy Beaumont finds a brain and then damages it! A sad moment for rugby football as Bill leaves the field for the last time in the 1982 county championship final at Moseley

With Bill Beaumont on his way to hospital, Terry Morris and myself hold the county championship trophy aloft in 1982

Me and Les Cusworth in jubilant mood after England had beaten Wales in 1982 at Twickenham

No wonder rugby players don't leave the pitch at half-time. The cabaret at half-time when England played Fiji at Twickenham in 1982

John Burgess makes a point in his own forceful style during his England coaching days

Mike Davis, an England coach who had total respect from all his players

Peter Colston, one of the embarrassingly long line of English coaches

Dick Greenwood. Good bloke, good captain, but little experience of coaching at the top level

The best coach I've ever been involved with at any level — Des Seabrook, talking to one of the great captains, Roger Creed

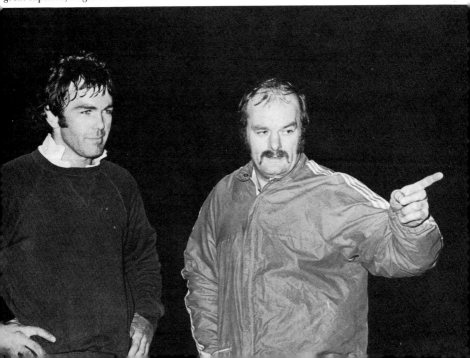

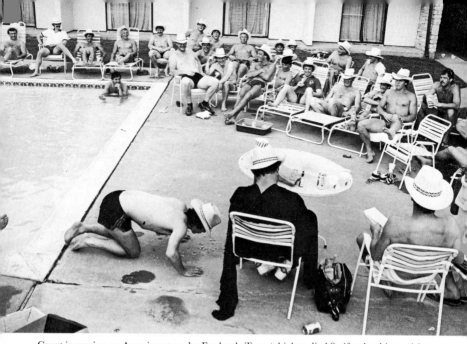

Court in session on American tour by England. Tony 'chicken dirt' Swift takes his punishment like a . . . man.

Settle down girls. Steve Bainbridge and USA flanker John Fowler trying to get acquainted without my permission

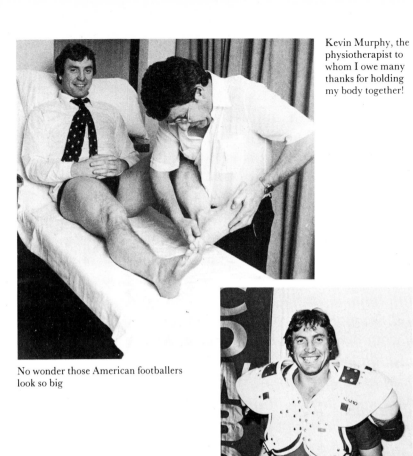

Kevin Murphy, the physiotherapist to whom I owe many thanks for holding my body together!

No wonder those American footballers look so big

Single-barrelled Smith talking to double-barrelled Smith. Myself with Nigel Starmer-Smith

My old pal Scotty launching me on another 'wobble' up the touchline. Later I launched John into England captaincy!

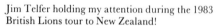

Jim Telfer holding my attention during the 1983 British Lions tour to New Zealand!

Leading out the Lions is an unbelievable experience

How I enjoyed my two Lions matches

To captain the North against the All Blacks at Gateshead in 1983 meant as much to me as captaining England and the Lions

Four ex-England captains watering the Bill Beaumont Rose. Tony Neary, myself, Fran Cotton and Bill, joined by grower, Alec Jenkins

I always enjoyed my battles with Terry Holmes

John Hipwell — a very fast but very short service

Facing Ireland's Colin Patterson, a scrum half I rated very highly

Jan Webster — best scrum half behind a beaten pack

Dave Loveridge — second in my list of scrum halves

Gareth Edwards — quite simply, 'The Best'

similar to that of the New Zealanders. Unlike the British, they don't see the game as a sport. They see it as a test of manhood. Personally, I like the way they play their rugby and the South Africans still treat the 1974 Lions as gods. When I was over there with North West Counties five years later, Fran and I were crossing a road when two cars screeched to a halt causing everybody else to stop. The drivers made a beeline for Fran just to shake his hand.

The one country I always seemed to miss out on was Australia. I should have gone there with the Penguins one year but the tour was called off and then I didn't get into the England side that made a disastrous tour of the country in the mid-seventies. My sole visit came about in an interesting way – more so when I reveal who instigated it. Geoff Nicholson, of the *Observer*, had asked me for an interview in 1980 and we had decided it would be a good deal more convivial if it was conducted over lunch at a pleasant restaurant in the Cheshire country-side.

We had just reached a point where I was telling him that one of the great things about playing rugby was being able to travel the world, when we were interrupted by a waiter who said someone was on the telephone to me from Australia. My face must have been a picture as I walked over to the telephone, placed it to my ear and the man at the other end introduced himself as David Lord. He was trying to organize a World XV to play in Sydney and wondered if I would like to play.

The only reservation I had concerned my travelling companion – Graham Price. I didn't know him very well and wondered what on earth I was going to talk about to a prop for thirty hours on a plane. He had always seemed a man of very few words, but I discovered that, like a lot of big men, he was quiet but when he opened up, he really opened up. He proved to be an intelligent and witty companion and we had an absolutely marvellous time Down Under. Of course, the first person I met up with was my old Loughborough buddy, John Gray, and

97

he made doubly sure we enjoyed ourselves. I also had a couple of nights out with David Lord, but that was a long time before his name became a household (some would say dirty) word in Rugby Union circles over his ambitious professional circus plan. He turned out to be a very sociable bloke who could charm the birds out of the trees.

The talented Hugo Porta was there to play fly half and the New Zealanders arrived in numbers, clearly intent on taking things seriously. I shared a room with Hika Reid, who would get up at the crack of dawn, go for a six-mile run, come back for breakfast and then go training. It was my practice to get up five minutes before training started and Pricey and I would then go through the session at a leisurely half pace whilst the New Zealanders were racing around at 100 miles per hour.

I got back to my room one day to find the beds had been moved and I said to myself, 'Cheeky old Hika, he's not as slow as I thought. He's been doing a little entertaining in here.' Then I jumped on the bed and something very hard stuck into my backside. On investigation I discovered a skipping rope handle. He'd moved the beds in order to do an hour's skipping!

It was a great game, which ended in a draw, and it gave me a particular thrill because it was played on the Sydney cricket ground. As we took the field one at a time so that we could be introduced individually to the spectators, I was able to imagine myself going out to open the batting for England in a Test match against the Aussies.

That was a fabulous summer for me because I visited Bermuda, Australia, South Africa and Zimbabwe. I was away so often and got so used to drinking cold, lager-type beers that I couldn't wait to get back to tackle a pint of Boddington's best bitter, the beer I had been weaned on. I trundled along to the Bridge Inn at Sale, quaffed my first mouthful and threw the rest away. I couldn't drink it and my mates thought I had been touched by the sun. Well, I haven't drunk a pint of bitter since, so that's what touring can do to you.

As I said at the beginning of this chapter, one of the nice things about the game is meeting personalities from other sports and being invited to interesting functions. In 1983 I was invited to speak at dinners in Vancouver, Kuwait and Dubai. The first two proved difficult because of business commitments, but I decided to take up the Dubai invitation and take the opportunity of doing some business for Bukta (the company I now work for) at the same time.

Originally I was to stay at the Dubai Hilton but I like to meet the natives and you don't meet them at the Hilton, unless, of course, you visit the London version. I was quite pleased, therefore, when I received a telex from a Colonel Paddy Manson asking if I would prefer to stay at his home instead. I accepted with my usual alacrity but wondered what sort of military gentleman he would turn out to be. He turned out to be a fantastic character and when I arrived at 3 a.m. the rugby lads were there to meet me and enjoy a few beers.

I was extremely well looked after and spent a lot of time at a country club used by the British community. One of the lads said he would arrange all my business appointments for the day before the dinner and I was all set to sell a few Bukta tracksuits, when he returned to say we couldn't conduct the interviews because the place was shut.

'What place?' I asked.

'Dubai,' he said.

Apparently one of the local sheik's wives had died and when they go into mourning they shut down the entire city. Although people were flying in from all over the Gulf for the dinner at which I was due to speak, the organizers decided the only thing they could do was cancel the event. They didn't want to offend local royalty. Could I, they asked, come back the following week?

Much as I would love to have done, I had to explain that my employer would doubtless view the whole thing very differently. But I did agree to return to speak the following year.

Another pleasurable diversion was being invited to take part in the television series, 'Superteams'. There was a time when I watched the 'Superstars' programme religiously but I stopped watching when superstars ceased to be average performers. Initially it was interesting to see people from different sports competing against each other over a wide range of sporting skills. Then we saw people with time on their hands starting to perfect a number of different skills and I suppose you couldn't blame professional sportsmen for trying to get their hands on a few thousand pounds that wouldn't normally have come their way. But I felt that approach killed much of the interest. Keith Fielding is a mate of mine and I would occasionally see him heading off to practise canoeing!

As the Rugby Union lads were unable to accept the money anyway they tended to take part just for a laugh, but it's one thing making a fool of yourself in front of ten people and a very different ball game doing it in front of ten million. 'Superteams' is a very different concept, however, and very enjoyable.

I've been involved in 'Superteams' a couple of times and the first year we had Fran as coach with a team comprising Jeff Squire, Graham Price, Ian McLauchlan, Phil Bennett, Nick Jeavons, Marcus Rose and myself. We got things worked out pretty well, leaving 'lovely legs' Jeavo and Rosie to do most of the grafting.

That year we tangled with the soccer lads before going on to the final where we beat the fighters. I think it is fair to say that none of our opponents have ever been able fully to understand our all-night training sessions. What you have to remember is that Bath is a very sociable city, the people who live there know who we are and it's open doors wherever you go. Quite apart from the fact that my sister and her family live in Bath, 'Superteams' was also an opportunity to get together with a few rugby mates such as my old adversary John Horton, Simon Jones and David Trick.

So, while we were going out in search of a little excitement and something to please the palate in the evenings, the fighters were having a team talk at nine and then going straight to bed. Mind you, they were being managed by Brian Jacks, who seems to spend his life eating, sleeping and talking 'Superstars' and eating oranges. I'll tell you, there's more fun in a Mars Bar.

Their coach was Jackie Pallo, the wrestler, a fabulous character who used to wander around with a bow in his hair. The lads in the team were great too, especially when we could get them away from Brian Jacks and their managers. I very quickly struck up a good relationship with former world champion Alan Minter and I enjoyed nothing better than sitting and listening whilst he talked about the fight game. Boxers have always amazed me but Alan reckoned we were crazier than they were. He said that at least they were skilled in the art of self-defence and could use that skill to ward off or ride an opponent's blows. That, he said, was rather more than we could do lying on a rugby pitch. As it can be murder down there, having sampled it, I suppose Alan had a point.

I also enjoyed a few cracks – not of the physical variety, let me hasten to add – with Dave Boy Green. On the first morning of events he approached me as we were about to board the coach taking us to the sports ground. He asked if we had been the noisy crowd that had returned to the hotel at about three that morning. I said it probably was because we had been out for a pretty wild evening, and he went off shaking his head. He couldn't believe it, bearing in mind that we were competing that morning. At that I called him back and told him that it didn't really matter how late we stayed out or how much we drank because the outcome was all in God's little book. Dave laughed and throughout the rest of the week kept asking me what was in the little book.

We were there to enjoy ourselves to the limit and to try to entertain the crowds, but Brian Jacks was tackling the

101

whole thing like a British Lions Test match. He seemed to spend his life practising for 'Superstars' and as he could handle a crossbow he was determined that that was one of the competitions the fighters would win – his confidence having been boosted by Fran's idea of coaching, which was to keep us out all night if possible. And that does not help your aim overmuch as it was sometimes difficult to hit your mouth with the first drink of the day.

The crossbow was one event none of us seemed to want to get involved in because we didn't want to look foolish on television, never having handled a crossbow before, let alone fired one. It was just beginning to look as though we would have to settle the issue by drawing lots when Graham Price, who had hardly spoken two words in four days, suddenly chipped in with, 'Don't worry boyoes. Squiresy and me'll do the crossbow. We Pontypool boys are good at blood sports.' Typical Pricey, he just picked up the crossbow, not a flicker of emotion on his face, and won the competition cool as you please. It was as easy as popping loose heads out of scrums.

In the end, the outcome depended on the last event, the tug-of-war, and Brian Jacks was really psyched up for that one. He was determined his lads were going to win and got on his high horse when there was some dispute over who should be allowed to take part. That was the worst thing he could have done because our lads were so annoyed they pulled the fighters three times out of three to win. The champagne came out back at the hotel and we all let our hair down, except Fran, who was camping it around the place with a bottle of bubbly in his big mitt and Jackie Pallo's bow in his hair.

The following year I tweaked my hamstring just before I was due in Bath but called in to say I couldn't take part. I was sitting having a coffee with Pricey and John Carleton when Roger Uttley, who was the manager, insisted that I stay on in some capacity. He decided I would have to be the coach and when I reminded him that Welsh coach, John Bevan, was travelling down to

102

take over that role, Mutters told me to leave everything to him. When Bev arrived, whistling happily and contemplating an easy four days, Roger broke the news that he was competing. His chin hit the deck.

Our semifinal opponents were the wheelies – drivers, cyclists and motorcyclists – and I was feeling a bit sorry for them as I had never heard of any of them before. I felt sorry until I saw the car park littered with Porsches and custom-built cars. Derek Bell, the great Le Mans twenty-four-hour driver, was telling me he had three Porsches, his wife had one and a new model was delivered every year. And to think Rugby Union lads got their wrists slapped for accepting a pair of Adidas boots every season!

Stirling Moss was the wheelies coach and he was a really nice bloke, as were the members of his team. It was interesting to chat to them and find out something about their particular sports. We were two strong for them in the end but there was one area of concern. The competition included a cycling relay and we felt it would be unfair if they included their two cycling champions unless they agreed to a scrum after each leg.

Anyway, the cyclists didn't take part and we agreed they could use a young lad who was the BMX champion. We hadn't the first idea what BMX meant but assumed it probably had something to do with motorbikes. He was due to ride the second leg and as we stood waiting I asked what he did. He explained he was the champion at doing tricks, twirls and somersaults on a push bike. I thought to myself, we've been stitched up here, and when I said so the lad simply shrugged and smiled as our first rider came in a few lengths down. Then it was my turn to laugh because this young champ leaped onto the bike, rode five yards and fell off. That was another event we won unexpectedly.

Our opponents in the final were the athletes and after the first day we decided the only way we were going to beat them was for each of us to grab an athlete and keep topping up his glass with champagne – which is always readily available at these events. Despite our valiant efforts we only succeeded in getting two of them pissed – hurdler Mark Holton and 400-metre runner Gary Cook – and dragged them out to visit a couple of nightclubs. They proved to be great lads and we all thoroughly enjoyed ourselves, but they were clearly less used to hard drinking than we were. The next morning they were really out of the game with king-sized hangovers. Gary also had tough luck because he went out to practise the cycling and went flying over the handlebars. He was lying in the road in an untidy heap and one wag cracked, 'Get him off the road before he gets breathalysed.'

It wasn't funny in the end because he had cracked his ribs and was out of athletics for a while.

We were no real match for the athletes but we enjoyed ourselves. For the four-man canoe race our lads dressed up as Mohicans, complete with headbands and war paint. Of course, Nick Jeavons wasn't keen because the headband was messing up his hair. We reckoned that Jeavo was the only swimmer who could do a tumble turn without getting his hair wet!

Another television programme I enjoyed was 'Question of Sport', which has my pal Bill Beaumont as one of the two captains. I have appeared on the programme twice, always on jockey Willie Carson's team, and each time was joined by a Liverpool footballer – Graham Souness and later Phil Thompson. Before the show, two episodes of which are filmed in one afternoon, you have a few beers and get to know one another. Willie, who is a nervous bundle of energy, told Graham and myself not to shout out any answers but to confer first by scribbling the answer on a pad. Once in front of the cameras, Willie kept shouting out all the wrong answers in his excitement and Graham and I had to tell him to shut up!

It was good competing with Bill because he really knows his sport. When we were away on tour together we would pass many an hour trying to catch each other out. My debut appearance on 'Question of Sport' ended perfectly. We needed to get the last question right to win and it was the one where you call a number, and are shown a photograph of a sporting personality in a weird pose. I called number six and a black mess came up on screen. Willie and Graham, looking quite desperate, admitted they hadn't a clue who it was, but I could see Billy B. groaning. I told the lads not to worry as I had been best man at his wedding and was godfather to his children. The picture was the one taken of Fran during the 1977 British Lions tour to New Zealand in which he looked as though he had been dipped in a mudbath!

Another time to laugh and remember. There have been many of those occasions too. Rugby Union can be fun because rugby is much more than just a game. It is a way of life and the fun and friendships are an important part of the whole. That, more than anything, sustained my interest, unwaveringly, even during the two years when England simply didn't want to know S. J. Smith.

8

Back with a Slam (1979–80)

The turning point in a career that seemed to be over so far as international involvement was concerned came when friend Fran damaged his Achilles tendon during the 1978–79 season. Off he went to Wrightington Hospital, near Wigan, for surgery and the surgeon told me afterwards that he had never seen bigger bones on a human being!

I wasn't exactly an advertisement for Nimble bread myself. My weight had shot up to just under 15 stone, a good deal of which seemed to have settled on my legs, backside and arms. I was still training, but I was also leading a pretty hectic social life and had lost all interest in playing for England again. County rugby still figured on my calendar but Cheshire weren't exactly lighting any fires and I didn't need to be a greyhound to figure prominently in that side.

Towards the end of that season the North West Counties announced that they would be going on tour to South Africa that summer, 1979, and I was asked if I would be available. Well, I don't normally have to be invited twice before leaping onto a plane to head to sunnier climes, but any thoughts of a purely fun tour went very quickly out of the window. The itinerary was extremely demanding and Fran, anxious to get back into shape for the tour following his operation, announced ominously that 'we' were going to get really fit.

Des Seabrook also took me on one side after the last game of the season between Sale and Orrell. I had toured America with Des, so knew him reasonably well and, having played scrum half with him at number 8, I realized that in addition to being a good footballer he also had excellent vision. Earlier that season I had sat on the bench when the North nearly toppled the All Blacks at Birkenhead Park. Des coached that side and I had been impressed with the way he had approached that game tactically.

The North were due to play the All Blacks again at Otley the following season and Des wanted to know how I felt about playing in the side. I told him I really wanted to have another crack at the New Zealanders, but the only way I was going to achieve that was by getting into a regional side. His suggestion was that I should aim for the North game and see what happened after that, which meant he was clearly looking farther ahead than I was.

It was quite obvious the North West Counties tour was intended to lay the foundations for the tilt at the All Blacks and what Des was telling me was that he would like me in there ... if. The 'if' was entirely up to me. Des said it would be a hard tour and if I was to help both the side and myself I had an awful lot of work to do on my fitness. It could, he said, be a make or break tour for me. How right he was.

The agony Fran had hinted at wasn't long in materializing. He told me in no uncertain terms – and he's not a man I'm inclined to argue with – that there would be nowhere for me to hide. When he came knocking at my door my only choice would be to get up, pull on a tracksuit and subject myself to one of his sadistic training sessions. The first three sessions were absolute murder. I was so physically shattered that I couldn't raise the energy to go out enjoying myself afterwards and I started to dread the sound of his mighty footsteps on the garden path, even though he was my pal.

It was Fran who came up with the solution to my dreadful suffering. I would, he decided, have to go on a diet and my lifestyle would have to change. With friends like that, who needs enemies!

Fortunately, the usual crop of lodgers at the Steve

Smith clearing house included the only female ever to have been allowed to stay there – Chris Broderick, who is now married to my pal Steve Rule, my halfback partner at Sale until he turned professional with Salford. Chris put me on a strict diet and told me I was going to stick to it.

That was something new for a start, a female giving me orders in my own house. She started cooking all the meals (I'm not as daft as I look) to make sure I ate only what the diet permitted (which wasn't much for a growing lad) and within two weeks my weight was down to 13 stone. I felt like a new man. It was a real slimline tonic because it affected my cricket. I hit three centuries for Brooklands and even my fielding improved.

My time at Loughborough had conditioned me to accept a lot of training and the new me got into the habit of training every day – a habit I have kept up ever since. Long runs became possible again and John Lansbury, a doctor at Sale who was with me in the North West side that beat the All Blacks at Workington, explained that my weight had caused the hamstring problems that made long runs difficult.

Once the weight was off I was determined to keep it that way and settled into a routine. I found that with daily training I could still enjoy the odd night out. If I had a real blow-out at the weekend, for instance, I wouldn't go out for the next couple of days, no matter how tempting the offer. The change in my fitness was such that when the North West squad met for a training session at Sale a week before departure, I had to put up with a lot of cracks from the lads when I appeared in the dressing room. My cheeks were hollow and I was an extremely skinny version of what I had been the previous season. The only problem was that I had been measured for my tour outfit before Fran put me on the treadmill and Chris attempted to starve me. By the time I picked up my kit everything simply hung from me. It's a good job Mother's a machinist; she was called on to take everything in.

The tour proved to be not just important in terms of my own comeback as an international player but also led directly to the revival of England's fortunes. Nobody should try to underestimate the importance of the tour party which included the nucleus of the North side that was to destroy New Zealand a few months later. Colin White, that marvellous prop from Gosforth, was there and I was delighted when he was finally honoured by England in the 1983–84 season.

Jim Syddall was a young lad taken for the experience and he came on like a bomb; John Carleton was starting to look like an international wing; Mike Slemen was there too and coming into his prime; while I was able to renew my old partnership with John Horton. Steve Bainbridge was another youngster taken for the experience and he was used as a number 8 – which is when I decided he would have to play second row!

Bill Beaumont led the party and he just got better and better as the tour progressed. He had Fran to help him. Then there was Peter Dixon, who was tremendous both on and off the field; Peter Williams, who played such an important role in Lancashire's success later, was undertaking his first big tour as deputy to John Horton; and John Basnett was developing his Rugby League skills! And it was on that tour that Des Seabrook was able to establish a style of play that was to have a major influence on English rugby and left me convinced he is the best coach in Britain.

The first game was against the Coloureds at Stellenbosch and the lads didn't play particularly well. I missed that one, Noel Byrne, from Liverpool, being given a run out, but I was in for the second match against Western Province at Newlands. They were just emerging as *the* team in South Africa and when I popped the ball into the first scrum our lads shot back about fifteen yards. Considering the talent packing down for us, I thought, Christ, this is going to be a hard afternoon.

That's when northern character took over and the side performed really well, even though we lost 13–12. When

109

a full-strength Cardiff played the same Western Province side they were thrashed by nearly 50 points.

We went on to beat Natal in Durban, lost narrowly to Orange Free State at Bloemfontein in what was a brilliant game of rugby, and our dirt-trackers lost to Transvaal when they should have won easily.

The tour ended on an extremely high note, however. We were lined up against a North Transvaal side that had been unbeaten for years but we ended their run with a tremendous 21–17 victory. That was our Test match and by the time I clambered aboard the plane for the homeward journey I had regained my old thirst for the game. I was also given some encouragement by Bill Beaumont, who had toured the Far East with England earlier that summer. He told me I was about tenth choice scrum half in the eyes of our national selectors, but, having seen the new slimline version in action in South Africa, he said he would be pushing for me as hard as he could.

Other moves were afoot by the time I got back to Sale. I had been contemplating a move of house to be nearer my office in Warrington – I was working for the Distributive Industries Training Board at the time – and Fran, always a major influence, told me I should make sure any move would take me into Lancashire so that I could play for a strong county side. We dug out an old Ordnance Survey map, spread it out on the kitchen table and set about trying to find a suitable spot within the Lancashire boundaries. We discovered that a brook which marked the boundary between the two counties ran across the bottom of my garden. You can imagine our amazement when we realized I had been living in Lancashire all the time. The irony of the situation was that Richard Kascow, Trevor Simon and John Gibson had all qualified to play for Cheshire by residing with me!

Fran, along with Lancashire's senior players, was very keen for me to make the county switch. So was Des, but I had mixed feelings about it. After all, I was Cheshire born, had played for the county at both cricket and rugby while at school and had become a fixture in the senior rugby 'side. When asked to be really honest, however, I suppose I had to admit that playing for Cheshire in those days was rather like banging your head against a brick wall. Cheshire didn't seem capable of improvement and were unbelievably inconsistent. The previous season we had beaten Yorkshire at Headingley and then lost to the worst Durham side I have ever seen. I was so annoyed by that performance I threw one of the committee out of the dressing room afterwards – and he had only come in to pay out expenses.

Cheshire were never going to be a top side. It wasn't due to lack of ability but to a lack of commitment. Playing for Cheshire didn't mean enough to the players, whereas anyone who has ever pulled on a Lancashire shirt knows the sense of pride derived from that simple act. The fact that a player wearing the familiar red and white strip might not be Lancastrian by birth doesn't seem to make the slightest difference when you lose. It still hurts like hell.

In a sense I was taking something of a gamble because my Cheshire place was virtually guaranteed and I would be challenging for a place in the North side from a secure base. Meanwhile, Waterloo's Dave Carfoot was well established in the Lancashire side and, despite what Des and Fran felt, my fate would be in the hands of the county selectors who were not certain to pick me rather than Dave. That didn't stop me making the switch though because I have always believed that if you are ever going to really achieve anything in this game of ours you have to be prepared to challenge the man in possession.

I wrote a letter to Cheshire and a couple of personal letters to explain why I was changing my allegiance, waited seven days for the fuss to subside and then hoped I would be selected to play for Lancashire in a warm-up game against Glasgow and District at Orrell. When the side was announced I was in, and pleased to see that my old pal Johnny Horton was to partner me. In the end he couldn't travel from Bath and Peter Williams, the Orrell fly half, was switched into the number 10 shirt, having originally been picked out of position in the centre as Tony Bond's partner. The hole in the centre needed plugging and the selectors turned to Tony Wright, who had joined Sale that season from Lymm, a local junior club. Tony was a marvellous little player who had been around for years but couldn't be tempted away from the junior game until quite late in his playing career. One can only wonder what he might have achieved had he taken the plunge earlier because he had so much to offer and was the perfect foil for Bondy's sabre thrusts. In a short space of time he achieved far more than most players dare dream of, and so far as Lancashire were concerned that season, Tony was the final piece in a fantastic jigsaw.

Having seen off Glasgow, we travelled by ferry to Belfast where we completely outplayed Ulster. The elation of the Sale contingent in the squad didn't last too long, however. Roger Creed, Fran, Tony Wright, Tony Bond, Ian McKie and myself had to take the night ferry to Scotland and from there faced a long drive to Wigton, in Cumbria, where Sale were playing in the John Player Cup. It was hardly the best preparation and Sale played like a bunch of old women. The junior club players showed tremendous spirit and determination and, with a good deal of help from us, caused one of the upsets of the competition by beating us. It was heartbreaking at the time but proved to be my only setback of the season.

After that we went straight into the old-style county championship and confidence flowed through the Lancashire side. The pack was in devastating form all season but that was hardly surprising with Cotton, Beaumont, Syddall, Creed and Neary in the line-up. And the backs were so sharp and bursting with flair and inventiveness that I knew an attack would be launched every time I let the ball out. Peter Williams had a marvellous season at fly half, probably the best he has ever had. At that stage

112

he seemed almost certain to develop into an international player but, although he made the England tour to Canada and America in 1982, his career seemed to lose some of its impetus after that season. Another player who had a great season was the Broughton Park fullback, Kevin O'Brien, who frequently came into the line with dramatic results; he worked extremely well in moves with Mike Slemen and John Carleton.

The first championship game was against Yorkshire at Bradford and that was an interesting challenge for me because I was up against Nigel Melville, an exciting schoolboy, who was being written up as a possible scrum half for the North side. It was believed that Budge Rogers, the chairman of England's selectors, was particularly keen for Nigel to play in the divisional side. That was the first time I had played against him and I could see he had a lot of talent; he turned out to be a great lad as well. He was on the wrong side that day, however, as Lancashire stuffed their great adversaries – even though the 15–6 scoreline didn't reflect the fact. We scored tries through Mike Slemen, Tony Wright and John Carleton, and I managed to have a hand in all three.

Faced with a challenge, I felt I had created the right sort of impression with the North game looming up. The only disappointment of that, my first Roses match, was Fran dislocating his shoulder; he expressed his usual forthright views later about the dangerous practice of dropping scrums. That put him out of action for most of the county campaign and cast a serious doubt over his availability for the All Blacks match.

Even without the cornerstone of our pack we still romped through the rest of the county campaign and it became a bad day if we didn't run in at least six tries, because double figures were nothing to those backs. The last game in the group was against Northumberland and as the Geordies had dented Lancashire's title hopes the previous season the lads were especially keen to do well. Fran eased himself back in gently, realizing he would have to prove his fitness to clinch a place in the North side. As things turned out, he didn't have to exert himself too much because the lads tore a good Northumberland side apart, with Kevin O'Brien enjoying the sort of afternoon attacking fullbacks dream about.

There had been rumours that Nigel Melville would be at scrum half in the North team, that Wakefield's Brian Barley would be in the centre and that Gosforth's Dave Johnson would be at fly half. But the North selectors were a shrewd bunch, resisted pressure from elsewhere and achieved the finest piece of selection I have ever seen. And not just because I was in the line-up. Tony Wright was alongside Tony Bond in the centre, despite having played no more than half a dozen senior club games, and Alan Old was at fly half. Anyone could have picked two thirds of that side but there were several crucial selections. One was the inclusion of Sale hooker Andy Simpson, even though he hadn't played county rugby that season. Another was the selection of Wrighty, as that meant the North was fielding the Lancashire threequarter line that was playing with great confidence and an uncanny level of understanding.

That North game at Otley was the only time that those three great back-row forwards, Roger Uttley at blind side, Peter Dixon at number 8 and Tony Neary at open side, have ever been picked in that order and it was a brilliant unit. Roger, although rarely playing in the position, had proved on the 1974 British Lions tour to South Africa how effective he was as a blind side, and while Peter Dixon was already accepted as a world-class flanker, he was the most underrated number 8 in the world.

The selectors had actually picked all the right players, people who were experienced and playing well, although a few eyebrows might have been raised at the inclusion of Alan Old. Everything we did in training was just right too. The sessions became shorter and shorter and the last session on the day before the game lasted a matter of minutes. We had a bit of a warm-up, passed the ball around for a spell, practised a couple of defensive lineouts and a couple of scrums. Then Des asked if there was anything we wanted to do. Any little thing we weren't happy with. But there wasn't anything because we had done it already. We were ready for the conflict. It was as smooth as that. In fact, it was so smooth it was worrying!

As we walked off the pitch the press gang was just arriving to watch us work out. They couldn't believe it when we said it was all over.

The build-up to the game was very different from the one at Workington where I had first faced the All Blacks. For one thing it was much quieter and more low key. John Burgess's success came partly from his ability to motivate players and get them psyched up. Des's success was based on having a superb team and knowing it. He knew we had the ability to beat the All Blacks at their own game and to do it even better than they could. In other words, we were good at driving at them, and at rucking and mauling tidily and efficiently. It was all very simple, basic rugby, with a northern commitment grafted on to match theirs. The North has always had a very high level of commitment and if the All Blacks ever doubted it they certainly know it now.

New Zealand rugby is very simple but is based on total commitment and total pride in what they are doing. Yet, although it is basically a simple game that they play, very few people can perform it at that high level. At Otley, Des had fifteen English players who could ... and did. Our plan was to play them at their own game with the emphasis on tying in their back row. That always has to be the first essential when you take on the All Blacks because their flankers fly off scrum, maul and ruck very, very quickly to put you under immediate pressure. At Otley they had Graham Mourie, Murray Mexted and Ken Stewart in the frame and that trio really was capable of creating total havoc. Yet, whenever I have played against them I have tended to have a good game, probably because I am required to run at them close, which suits my game. They don't like being tied in and would rather you ran the ball wide, especially in your own half or from set pieces, when they can really put you on the rack.

Even if you succeed in breaking their first line of defence there is such a wave of black shirts coming across to cut you off that you are never going to get through the second line. They are so effective at it that I would defy anyone to say they have seen many tries scored against them from a long way out.

But our planning for the game was meticulous, even down to the kit we wore. When it was handed out to us the day before the game we felt ten feet tall. Too often with these games there is no identity to the strip and you have to hand it back afterwards. That strip was ours to keep and it was the nearest thing you are ever going to find to a British Lions strip. The main difference was the English rose on the breast where the Lions badge normally goes. Mind you, as Fran and I pulled on those beautifully tailored Bukta shirts, we never thought that one day we would end up working for the company that made them.

So, everything was perfect and that's why it was probably the quietest build-up to an important game that I can recall. I was completely confident we were going to beat them and the atmosphere that day was such that there was no need for anyone to go around beating a drum.

The All Blacks side was: Richard Wilson; Bernie Fraser, Gary Cunningham, Mark Taylor, Stu Wilson; Eddie Dunn, Mark Donaldson; Brad Johnstone, Andy Dalton, John Spiers, Andy Haden, John Fleming, Ken Stewart, Murray Mexted, Graham Mourie.

The North line-up: Kevin O'Brien (Broughton Park); John Carleton (Orrell), Tony Wright (Sale), Tony Bond (Sale), Mike Slemen (Liverpool); Alan Old (Sheffield), Steve Smith (Sale); Colin White (Gosforth), Andy Simpson (Sale), Fran Cotton (Sale), Bill Beaumont (Fylde), Jim Syddall (Waterloo), Roger Uttley (Wasps),

Peter Dixon (Gosforth), Tony Neary (Broughton Park).

Referee: Alan Hosie (Scotland).

One thing you can be sure of with the All Blacks is that they will try to put you under pressure right from the start. From the kick-off, Billy took the ball and drove into their pack. Things started to fly and Billy, as usual, was the last to haul himself off the ground, having been paid close attention by Murray Mexted. At that point Fran grabbed hold of Mexted and warned him, 'If you do that again, I'll kill you.'

Fran's chin was down to his knee caps and even though he was on my side he scared me. But Murray just turned to him and said, 'You've got eighty minutes to do it, Cotton.'

I remember thinking that people simply couldn't say that sort of thing to big Franny but that incident just about summed things up. It typified the total commitment oozing out of both sides.

When we got down to the rugby, however, we had a very definite edge. It's terribly important really to knock the All Blacks over in the tackle and that's exactly what we did. Tony Bond in the centre got in a succession of bone-rattling tackles on Taylor and Cunningham, and J.C. (John Carleton) got in a few belters too. Our back-row trio wasn't exactly backward at tackling either, and instead of driving towards our line with the back row in close support, our opponents were being smacked right back on their arses. Given that power base, we had our own marvellous rucking forwards and there can have been few displays anywhere to match that of Nero, Dicko and Mutters that day.

Alan Old got us on to the scoreboard with a penalty steered through a wind that was so strong Nero had to steady the ball for him. Then, with the game thirty-two minutes old, I scored one of the most important tries of my entire career. Because of the wind it was very difficult for Alan to kick wide, so most of the early kicking was left to me. I drilled one along the deck towards the corner. The Wilsons got into a mix-up as Slem followed up brilliantly to sweep up the ball and fling it back inside to enable me to take it and scamper over the line. It was a marvellous moment.

After the interval we had the wind at our backs and there was no holding us. We pummelled away at the New Zealand line with our forwards winning their personal battles in every phase. With the pressure on, Tony Bond burst through for two great tries, and Alan Old jinked over for a fourth when our pack got their opposite numbers into all sorts of trouble at a scrum close to their line. Admittedly, the All Blacks staged their usual strong finish with a goal and a penalty but it was purely academic. We had scored four tries to one and given the All Blacks a thoroughly good hiding. Significantly, Graham Mourie said afterwards that it had been the most comprehensive defeat he had known as an All Blacks captain.

It was one of the most important victories in the history of English rugby and what annoyed me, and still does, is the way the victory simply disappeared. Instead of people beating the drum, it was hardly mentioned afterwards. It was almost as though it had never happened; the only person who still refers to it and clearly realized its significance is John Reason of the *Sunday Telegraph*. During the 1980 British Lions tour to South Africa John told me he thought it had been the greatest victory this century.

'Thank God, somebody has said it,' I replied. 'I was beginning to think the game had never been played and that I must have dreamed it.'

I have no doubt that the North's performance at Otley resurrected my international career. Before the game the indications had been that Ian Peck, who had toured the Far East with Chris Gifford, would be at scrum half, and even though the selectors obviously shuffled the cards after Otley, they still didn't go far enough. Fran's dad tells the story of seeing Budge Rogers scurrying away to his car after the game to drive to the selection meeting and a little old northerner, in a flat cap, rushing across to the car, opening the middle page of his programme and waving it under Budge's nose, shouting, 'There's the bloody team, Rogers. Now get it picked.'

That night I was told by Burge that I definitely wasn't in the England team. I wasn't too bothered at hearing that because I had achieved what I set out to do, but it wasn't the greatest thing to tell me, especially as my mother burst into tears. If she had got into the selection meeting at that moment I wouldn't have given much for their chances!

As you might imagine, we had a pretty wild night and it was a happy, but weary, breakaway party that had to drive to Leicester the following morning for an England session. We sat in the dressing room, still half hung-over, as they read out the team to play New Zealand that Saturday and, total surprise, I was in.

I don't know what had gone on in selection but they had got it partly right. They still made two crucial errors though in picking Les Cusworth and Mike Rafter. I'm not knocking either player when I say that, but the selectors had failed to understand all the message we had hammered out at Otley. The game they needed to play just wasn't Les's game at that time. He had always played very well with the Leicester lads and was very definitely a play-maker. But against the All Blacks you have to concentrate on getting deep into their half and Les wasn't a big kicker – Paul Dodge and Clive Woodward tended to do a lot of the kicking at Leicester. As we didn't have a kicker in the centre that role was left to Les, who couldn't handle it, instead of the job being given to the player who had proved he could do it, Alan Old.

Roger Uttley's omission was a terrible blow. I've got enormous respect for Mike Rafter, he's a superb player and a great bloke, but he was being asked to play a game more suited to Roger's talents. Fran and Nero have never been fully replaced in the England side but the gap left by Roger was even greater. Not many players can work as effectively behind the number four in the lineout as

119

Roger could; Wales experienced a similar sense of loss when Jeff Squire bowed out of the international arena. Roger had superb hands and would often end up winning more lineout ball than the jumpers.

So, although we had the chance to beat New Zealand at Twickenham, it became a stalemate, boring game. I was very impressed by Dave Loveridge, who was playing opposite me, and Graham Mourie was clearly determined to salvage All Blacks pride in the wake of their defeat at Otley. Richard Wilson put them in front with a penalty early in the game and then Loveridge hoisted a beauty into the box. It dropped over the line and bounced straight back into the arms of New Zealand lock, John Fleming, who was left with the simple task of dropping over the line. Dusty Hare and Richard Wilson exchanged penalties before half time and we turned round 7 points adrift. Dusty landed two more penalties to put us right back into the game but it was a stop-start affair and I suppose the All Blacks just about deserved to win on the day's performance by virtue of having scored the game's only try. The score was England 9 New Zealand 10.

The defeat was a blow to our hopes and disappointing to those of us who had beaten them so comprehensively just seven days previously. It was frustrating too because we all knew England should have beaten them, but the selectors hadn't got the line-up quite right and Mike Davis, as coach, hadn't got the thing together. Not that I am knocking Mike because I came to respect him both for his ability and as a person. At that time, however, I think he would be the first to admit, being the honest individual that he is, that he was very raw at senior coaching.

He had moved straight from the England Schoolboys job and it was one hell of a gap to bridge. On the Far East tour he had established a good rapport with the lads, especially Billy, but he was suddenly confronted by players of the calibre of Fran, Nero and Peter Wheeler, not all of whom had been on the tour. To be honest, I think he was rather awed by their presence and by the fact that he was suddenly dealing with players he didn't know. He was also a prime target to be knocked. After all, the northern contingent had their own favourite coach in Des and the Leicester lads had wanted Chalkie White as England coach – a not unnatural desire.

It is interesting to compare the game in 1983 when we beat New Zealand at Twickenham. The selectors turned to the Midlands side that had already exposed All Black weaknesses. That probably cost me another cap because Nick Youngs was chosen along with four other Leicester backs, but I couldn't argue with the decision. The lads proved on the day that they were the men for the repeat performance and that's exactly what should have happened in 1979.

It was an unhappy start for Mike but his strength was that he was a good learner. His other qualities were that he was a good bloke anyway, very honest and a good selector (and there weren't too many of those around). He also had the ability to get on with people. Budge wasn't the easiest man to get along with but Mike seemed to be one of the few able to persuade him to change his rather set attitudes. Mike was well liked and that is nearly nine tenths of the battle. After the All Blacks defeat I think he realized, as the senior players did, that all the selectors had to do was pick the right side and we could pull off the Grand Slam.

As history shows, we were right, but none of us really got to know Budge during that season, which is unusual when you are involved in a group enjoying great success. He was always quiet and aloof. I certainly didn't know what he was like beneath the veneer, not that players and selectors chat over much.

I talked to Mike quite a lot, however. As a scrum half it has always been my policy to try to work with people and I always got on very well with Billy, for instance. His role that season was really strange; at his early team talks you could see he was almost embarrassed to be standing there. I certainly didn't envy him his position. In the pack were Fran, Wheelbrace, Mutters and Nero, who had either been, or should have been, captain of England already, so it was a tremendous challenge for Bill. Fortunately, he was such a fantastic player and is such a marvellous man that he got away with it. He related very well to me but was almost too embarrassed to talk to that great quartet. After all, Fran and Nero were already established as world-class players when young Bill made his Lancashire debut.

It says a lot for Bill's ability and honesty that every single player gave him full support that season. The great quartet was prepared to do anything for him ... and did. So far as they were concerned, he was the leader and they acted as his senior generals. It was marvellous; for once England had a sprinkling of world-class players and you felt humble in their presence. I suppose the situation was similar to that of Wales a few years previously when the nucleus of the side was a class apart.

Although I was involved in it and perhaps shouldn't say it, I think a key factor that season was the relationship between Bill and myself. We had always got on as mates off the field and we transferred that relationship to the area of combat. Bill was the boss and he led by example but he spent a lot of his time stuck in scrums, rucks and mauls and relied on me to get things organized at the back. Any successful side has to have a scrum half who makes the right decisions and I think I managed that role in 1980.

The first game was against Ireland and by that time the selectors were on the right track. They called up John Horton to partner me, brought in Roger at blind side and, one of the key selections, drafted in Phil Blakeway at tight-head and switched Fran to loose-head.

Ireland were being tipped to win the title and they got off to a marvellous start at Twickenham. Although Dusty kicked an early penalty, Ollie Campbell rifled over three beautiful kicks to give Ireland a 9–3 lead. I remember standing under the posts with Fran and saying to him that Ollie wasn't merely getting them over, he was hitting every one straight through the middle. It was a remarkable display of precision goal kicking.

By contrast, I was having a terrible opening spell. I put two kicks directly into touch and felt I was really blowing it. Things were so bad I told myself to get a grip, stop kicking for touch and get things moving. With that pack in front of me the ball was coming back as though it were on a conveyor belt and I decided to keep putting it back in front of them so they could keep churning forward. For ten minutes Ireland never saw the ball. Everytime I got my hands on it I broke close to work with the back row or fed it out to Johnny, who was one of the best kickers of the up-and-under I have ever seen. He did it so well I almost felt sorry for my Lancashire pal Kevin O'Brien who was making his Irish debut and being subjected to a baptism of fire.

The pack produced a splendid spell of pressure and after winning a series of rucks I was able to dart over for our first try. We were just a yard out when Fran ripped the ball out and gave it to me. I went to drive really hard for the line and almost fell over and dislocated my shoulder because the anticipated cover wasn't there. We had succeeded in sucking in so many players that my mother could have scored that try.

The only upset that afternoon came when my Sale team-mate, Tony Bond, broke his leg. It was a sickening moment and a great disappointment for Bondy who had worked so hard to get into the side. He was replaced by Clive Woodward, from Leicester, and that didn't turn out to be such a bad replacement!

That disruption didn't slow our momentum, either. I put a kick into the corner, which Kevin failed to clear properly, and Mike Slemen was on it in a flash to score a try. John Scott got the third with a back-row move we had worked out between us and which produced a number of scores that season – even though Budge criticized us for doing it.

Scotty really developed into a class number 8 that season, but he got a mother and a father of a rollicking from the senior statesman during the Irish game. We had planned a scrum move that involved me picking up and feeding Nero but, when we tried it, Scotty got in on the act and fouled everything up. Now, Scotty is never short of a word or two, especially in his own defence, but Nero really laid into him. John, realizing who was talking to him, kept his mouth shut and got his act together. It did him no harm having Nero, Roger and myself telling him what to do.

Anyway, Dusty slotted a few kicks and Ireland were a well-beaten side. We had turned a 9–3 deficit into a 24–9 victory so our spirits were very high, even though our next daunting task was to tangle with the French in Paris. I had a feeling we might just be all right though. The last time I had been over there we had been whitewashed and as the game approached I have never seen Fran so psyched up. If we were going to avenge that humiliating defeat, then this was going to be the game and the lads sensed it.

The French are always so totally unpredictable, of course, and when Jean-Pierre Rives scored a try in the first five minutes my heart sank into my boots. As I stood behind the posts waiting for the conversion attempt, I thought, Oh no. Not again.

The bands were playing, the fire crackers were going off, horns were blowing and it was a very lonely spot for an Englishman. People talk about Cardiff Arms Park putting the fear of God into players, but there is no more daunting stadium than Parc des Princes in Paris. Playing there gets the involuntary muscles in your backside going at a great rate of knots, I can tell you.

Dusty kicked a penalty to cut the lead to 1 point – the conversion attempt having failed – but we then conceded a penalty that gave France the chance to restore the 4-point margin. And the conceding was done by Fran.

It was an interesting incident because a scrum broke up with Fran flattening Robert Paparemborde, the French prop. Referee Clive Norling called Fran over while the crowd bayed for him to be sent off and Clive delivered a stiff lecture. That was the only comment made on the incident. Normally Billy would have gone across to the player concerned and given him a rollicking, but you never spoke to Fran when he was in that mood. Half an hour went by before I could pluck up the courage to ask my old pal if he was all right. Fran just turned round and snarled, 'If he does that again, he'll get another one.' He was still psyched up to the eyeballs. I don't know what Pap had done and I wasn't about to ask!

Nick Preston worked his way over for a try and then Scotty and myself worked our little back-row move to put John Carleton in for his first championship try. That was the move that had prompted Budge to comment that he didn't know why we bothered trying it because it never led to a score. Well, little did he notice because that was two in as many games. The match clincher, however, was Johnny Horton, who dropped two magnificent goals; his role in the championship was greatly underestimated. John had a truly marvellous season and was a vital cog in the England machine.

Afterwards we celebrated long and hard and the minute we arrived at the post-match reception Fran declared, 'Right, we can drink with them now.' That was a reference to the previous debacle and we certainly worked that one out of our systems as we tackled Paris by night. At one stage we ended up in a nightclub and nobody knew who we were. A floor show was going on involving about twenty effeminate waiters whose party trick was to turn round and reveal bare backsides. Then, suddenly, Fran and Nero appeared on stage doing their version of the can-can, which had the lads falling about. Well, can you imagine it, two macho males like that pair cavorting around like a couple of baby elephants whilst the 'puffy' waiters battled gallantly to carry on their routine as though nothing else was happening.

Eventually, our heroes were dragged into the wings, Fran fluttering his eyelashes and falling back in mock horror every time one of the waiters tried to put a hand on him. The bewildered audience was trying to decide whether to laugh or cry when our undaunted pair suddenly reappeared doing a wheelbarrow across the stage and waving at the crowd. It was absolutely hilarious. Of course, the night club wasn't one of your backstreet fleshpots. Everyone wore evening dress and the champagne was flowing as quickly as the money out of the punters' pockets. They all stood and applauded when it was announced that the surprise cabaret was provided by members of the England team. It was a wild night which continued into day and it was an extremely well-watered Steve Smith who arrived back home in time to pop into the local for a nightcap, clad in Rives's shirt.

The week before the Paris game I had a journalist from *Paris Match* in tow who had travelled to England to write an article about me. He attended the England session at Stourbridge and as we rode back with Fran and Nero he asked our thoughts on the coming French game. It was then we realized that within three weeks we would have played against France, played for Lancashire in the county championship final and tackled Wales at Twickenham. All three were terribly important to us but we decided we couldn't possibly win every one. Conversation got around to which two we would most like to win, not for a minute believing we could actually win all three.

I have never known three weeks like it with the actual games, squad sessions and the attendant mental build-up and physical recovery afterwards. People talk about introducing a World Cup for rugby but, with the demands of top-class rugby these days, it would probably finish off a few of us for good.

The county final was held at Vale of Lune on a day more suited to ducks. Some scribes concentrated more on a pig that joined the throng of spectators on the rain-lashed hillside overlooking the ground, than on the field of action.

The match itself was absolutely incredible because Lancashire confidence and understanding had reached such a high level that we played dry-weather rugby on a quagmire with a ball that resembled a bar of soap. Kevin O'Brien, more relaxed than on his Irish debut, skated through the Gloucestershire cover for two great tries, while J.C. and Slem got one each. Although Nigel Pomphrey burst through for a late consolation try to produce a more respectable 21–15 scoreline, the outcome was never in the slightest doubt. Yet, credit must go to the West Country lads for helping to make it a memorable game.

That was two down and one to go in terms of our high-pressure trio of games. The big question then was whether we could raise ourselves to beat Wales and make the Grand Slam a serious possibility. Unfortunately the game was built up to such an extent that we almost expected Clint Eastwood to walk out of the sunrise with his guns slung low. The press went a bit over the top and a war of hatred – hatred that didn't exist – was stirred up. There were even daft suggestions that the Welsh were going to make the English pay for miners being laid off in the Welsh coalfields. Utter nonsense, but it certainly achieved a nasty atmosphere if that was the intention. In all the internationals I have played over the years there has always been a fairly friendly atmosphere. You feel it in the hotel and the streets before the game. You feel it when you arrive at the ground and even during a game. But at Twickenham that day there was an atmosphere, as we ran on to the pitch, that was electrifying. It was very different from the normal high-spirited crowd and there was a feeling of hatred coming from what seemed to be a seething mass of people. There was no real cheering as you would normally expect, and the whole experience chilled the blood.

I'll never forget putting the ball into the first scrum. As the rival front rows went down nobody aimed for the gap and there was such a crack that I thought someone had fired a cannon. It was mayhem from first to last and poor old Roger Uttley had his face ripped wide open by Geoff Wheel's boot. It was the worst facial injury I had ever seen, but, in spite of all that was going on, I'm convinced it was an accident with Geoff aiming for the ball, missing and catching Roger.

Off went Roger to be replaced by Mike Rafter (who could have been excused for declining the call) and it became simply a matter of time before someone was sent off. As things turned out it was Paul Ringer, for what was a fairly innocuous incident but one which came almost immediately after referee Dave Burnett had issued a general warning. Dave had little choice after that. It was just before the incident that Billy got hold of us and told us not to do anything stupid and hold our tempers.

Ironically, Wales could have won that game had they stayed cool. After all, Gareth Davies gave one of the finest kicking displays by a fly half that I have ever seen and even though Wales spent a long time playing with only fourteen players we never really gained any advantage. Dusty kicked a penalty for the Ringer incident, a late tackle on Johnny Horton, but there was a mix-up at the back of a scrum and Jeff Squire dived through to score. Dusty put us in front again and then came the incident that hit me in the solar plexus.

Time was running out and I made a good clearing kick down the left touchline. A few seconds later I tried the same thing only to see Alan Phillips, the Cardiff hooker, charge it down and burst down field before sending Elgan Rees in for a try to put Wales 8–6 ahead. I have never, in all my life, felt as I did at that moment. It is the only time when I could hold my hand on my heart and say I had lost my bottle. As I trooped back over the England line I couldn't bring myself to look my team-mates in the eye. I felt I had betrayed them all and went to squat alone on my haunches in the corner whilst Gareth prepared to take the conversion. With the rest of the side gathered disconsolately behind the posts, I felt like a leper. That was until Billy spotted me and, being the great man that he is, ambled slowly across to me. He wrapped his big, teddy-bear arm around my shoulders, pulled me towards him and whispered, 'You stupid little bastard.'

That's the story that is told with relish in rugby circles but, of course, if you believe that, you'll believe anything. Bill, fabulous guy that he is and always has been, simply told me not to worry about it – which says a great deal for a character whose hopes of glory looked as though they had been totally destroyed.

Luckily for England, and me in particular, Gareth was off target with the conversion attempt and, miraculously, we were offered a thread to clutch on to when Wales were penalized in injury time. As Dusty walked casually up to the spot where the offence had been committed I said a little prayer. I looked up at the heavens and said, 'Dear God, if there is any justice, please let him kick this.'

As the history books show, Dusty produced what I regard, for personal reasons, as the kick of the century to win the game for us. I ran towards him to tell him how great I thought he was and he was wobbling back as calmly as if he had been to put the kettle on for tea. I used to have a little joke about Dusty that he spent his time writing postcards back there in his territory and broke off occasionally to catch a high kick or take a pot at goal. As I watched him wobble back into our 22, I thought, He's going to finish that postcard.

The England dressing room afterwards was like a battleground. There was a queue of about eight England players waiting to have stitches in an assortment of cuts; I was last in line because I only needed three in a cut beneath my left eye. Typically of rugby though, the lads mixed together after the game and nobody mentioned what had gone on earlier. We simply sank a few beers and I remember joining the Welsh lads in a singsong at one stage. The players of both sides had been the innocent victims of the build-up to the game. The whole affair had become political and, at the end of the day, had absolutely nothing to do with rugby. It was the one blemish of the Grand Slam campaign, although, having said that, I think it is the element of violence that attracts many people to the game. It's sad when the violence

129

spills over to that degree but at least it's better than going to war. If the Welsh feel like going to war with the English over pit closures I still think it's better that they kick hell out of us on a rugby pitch rather than start shooting at us.

We had a month's break before the final game against Scotland and we definitely needed it. After the Welsh match I felt as though I had flu. Every bone in my body ached. Physically, it was the hardest game I have ever played in. Every time you ended up on the grass you were stamped on and by the end of the game I wasn't quite sure who was doing the stamping. The close-quarters stuff was quite horrific and there are times, even now, when I watch internationals on television and think, God, do I play that?

Perhaps it is the hardness of the game that makes us drink. We sink a lot of beer after a match and it works as an anaesthetic on the pain. You also get so psyched up for a big game that you take the thumps and bumps without really feeling them. I think the psyching up that day caused people to do things they wouldn't normally dream of doing. I remember Steve Fenwick thumping somebody on the blind side of a ruck. Now, Steve's a great guy and that action was totally out of character. Terry Holmes had a go at his Cardiff team-mate, John Scott, and that's not Terry. The effect of the game on the Welsh boys was tremendous and when I toured some time later with Jeff Squire he told me they had never recovered from it that season. They were mentally and physically finished.

I suppose we had the best tonic in the world in the realization that only Scotland stood between us and the Grand Slam. That had almost become the unattainable for England who hadn't achieved it since another Sale and Lancashire player, Eric Evans, led the rose to that distinction back in 1957. As the final match approached it seemed as though everyone in England was willing us to win and Bill became the most sought-after personality in the country. Having sampled captaincy myself, I honestly don't know how he coped with all the attention.

By the time we reached our team hotel, the Peebles Hydro, Mike Davis had grown in confidence to such an extent that he really was taking the squad sessions. He had developed into the boss man, enjoying the respect and support of the players, and Billy was very much the governor on the field. He had grown ten feet tall and we all walked with our chests out and our chins up. So different from the old days when we didn't want to go home or be seen for a week.

Our stay at the Hydro was marvellous and we trained with the beautiful Scottish hills as our backcloth. I suppose Mike should have been slipping something into our tea to slow us down a little because we were training at 100 m.p.h. The truth is, we were rested, we were hungry and we wanted success. We were going to get it too and there wasn't the slightest doubt about that in the England camp. It must have been akin to the mood of the Welsh during their great Grand Slam seasons and, as with the North game against the All Blacks, we were prepared and ready. At Murrayfield, the crowd was expectant. The English fans got what they wanted and the Scottish fans witnessed a game that erased the memory of the Welsh battle.

Johnny Horton had another fine kicking game and the pack would tell you that every time they looked up we were going forward. We ripped into the Scots like an express train and had stormed into a 19–3 lead by half time. There was no doubt we were going to win and handsomely. John Carleton scored a magnificent hat trick – one of them following the Scott–Smith move that never produced tries – and Clive Woodward turned in his most mesmeric performance yet. Mike Slemen scored a try and I finished off a move involving Bill, Roger Uttley and Scotty, to make sure all five tries had been scored by members of the Lancashire team. As I walked back upfield I caught sight of my father sitting in the stand and I thought back to those days when he stood on the touchline in his motorcycling gear. Unlike some of the people at the game, he wasn't there just for the Grand Slam. He had been there from the start.

We let ourselves get carried away a little and the Scots came back at us. But we finished two clear scores ahead and nobody would deny that we were the men of the hour. Oddly enough, it was a strange evening with the jubilation rather supressed. That may have been because it was a time for reflection, especially for those who had been around for a long time. Normally I would spend a few minutes with my parents after a game and then rejoin my mates at the bar. But that night I was with my parents and sister Susan for a couple of hours. We are a close family, without being overemotional, but I felt I wanted to shut myself up with them after what had to be the climax of a career they had followed, unfailingly, from my early schooldays. That night, I felt, belonged just as much to them too.

Even when we drove home the following day, Fran and I went to one of our local haunts, the Bull's Head at Poynton, for a few drinks with friends. We both had the feeling of wanting to be with people we knew. We had spent the last few weeks in a goldfish bowl and on a pedestal. Now we wanted to be back on terra firma.

It was over a quiet pint that I reminded Fran that the Grand Slam team had been around for five seasons. Apart from Clive Woodward, we had all been available, and I thought back to the combined North and Midlands side that defeated Argentina at Welford Road, Leicester, in October 1976. The back division that day was Hare; Carleton, Dodge, Bond, Slemen; Horton, Smith. Up front were Wheeler, Cotton, Beaumont and Neary, while players like Peter Dixon and Roger Uttley were seasoned internationals by that time.

That was the occasion when Dicky Jeeps told us off for playing in a negative style. What he overlooked was the fact that it was a winning style. The players were always available if only the selectors had picked them and the sad thing about the Grand Slam side is that it started to break up before the success could be repeated.

9

Farewell to Friends (1980–82)

One of the things I have discovered about sport, and life in general, is that you're not allowed to stay up on cloud nine for too long. Some of the close friends who travelled the same hard, obstacle-strewn, frustrating road to the Grand Slam were soon to leave the stage. They would do so without proper recognition of what they had achieved because the RFU surprisingly acted as though they were almost embarrassed by the success. The lads would have loved some small, spontaneous token to commemorate the feat, but, although Budge had promised us blazer badges before the French game, nothing happened. In fact, we had to wait a year before there was any recognition whatsoever and then we were presented with a team photograph – by the groundsman at Twickenham.

During the tour of Argentina in 1981 some of us had a real go at RFU secretary, Bob Weighill, and RFU trustee, Mickey Steele-Bodger, about it. Mickey didn't want to hear but Bob did appear to listen and I suspect he was responsible for the players receiving a beautiful Grand Slam tie some time later. The sad thing is that not everyone who played that season received one.

I would hate people to assume the lads want a great deal from rugby. They don't in spite of the time and energy the game demands of them and the inconvenience it subjects them to. But small gestures often mean a great deal to the players concerned. Of course, we were besieged with things from other people, ranging from mugs and ties to shirts and sweaters.

It was after the Grand Slam campaign that I first started to have doubts about Budge. He was England's representative on the British Lions selection panel and only eight members of our side were chosen for the party to tour South Africa. Had it been a Welsh Grand Slam side they would probably have gone en bloc.

I was disappointed, although not terribly surprised, when Terry Holmes and Colin Patterson were chosen ahead of me at scrum half. They were extremely talented and I knew I would have to produce something special to push one of them out of the way. But I was bitterly disappointed when John Robbie was called up as a replacement for Terry Holmes. He was a good player but hadn't played for Ireland for three seasons.

To get over yet another disappointment I took myself off to Zimbabwe with a Lions reject side and on my return was doing some preseason training when Garth Ormond, who lives in the same house, drove up and told me to hop into the car. As he drove me home he said I was being flown out to South Africa as a replacement for the last Test because Colin Patterson was injured. I immediately called John Lawrence, secretary of the Four Home Unions, who told me the choice of replacement would be between myself and Brynmor Williams. They hadn't quite made up their minds but I was to stay close to a telephone.

I cancelled my night out but didn't tell my folks in case it didn't come off as there seemed no point in them being disappointed unnecessarily. All evening I sat waiting and the hours ticked by. When midnight arrived I told myself I wasn't going and decided to call John Lawrence so that he could put me out of my misery officially. I actually got him out of bed and to my amazement he told me I was going and said I had to be at the South African Airways check-in desk at Heathrow at a certain time the following day. I still wonder what would have happened if I hadn't bothered to call him!

Anyway, I trained that morning, threw some things into a bag and took the shuttle to London. When I got to the check-in desk there was nobody there to meet me so I simply picked up the ticket. The first time I came into contact with any sort of official was when we landed at Jan Smuts Airport. It's a good job I had become something of an experienced traveller; I've often wondered since how a young player, making his first trip overseas, might have coped.

At the hotel I met up with all the lads and, of course, we all had a good laugh together. You can imagine the sort of thing, typical of Smithy to pop over for the weekend. The laughing stopped when tour manager Sid Millar came up to my room and asked if I had got my Lions gear. I told him he had to be joking as I hadn't seen a soul and he then did a fair impression of someone going completely bananas.

As things turned out I had four great days; there was a marvellous spirit in the camp, although they were 3–0 down in the Test series. It was then I realized what a tremendous job Billy Beaumont had done out there. He called me up to his room for a chat, but it was impossible to talk because the telephone never stopped ringing. Bill, being the sort of bloke he is, had to chat to everybody who wanted to bend his cauliflower ear. In the end we had to retire to the sanity of my room. He said that sort of mayhem had been going on for ten weeks. How on earth he coped with that sort of pressure, played so well and held the party together I'll never know, but I don't think I could have done it.

The lads certainly appreciated what he had done and there was no way they were going to let him return to Britain as the captain of a whitewashed side. They were really psyched up for the last Test and I was as delighted as everybody else when they won. I sat on the bench alongside coach, Noel Murphy, who is a smashing guy, and he said that if the Lions were well ahead with five minutes to go he would do his best to get me onto the field. I declined his kind offer though; there had been hundreds of Lions but only one who had never got onto the field. Me.

135

About two weeks later all my Lions gear arrived at home but I wouldn't wear it because I didn't feel like a proper Lion. I gave the shirt away, but, being a practical lad, I thought it would be a shame to waste the blazer so I took it to my mother and asked her to remove the badge.

As she started to take it off the badge began falling apart and poor Mum was nearly in tears. When my dad arrived home and opened the back door the tattered remains of a British Lions badge whistled past his ear and he ended up chasing the remnants all over the garden.

When I was on a tour with Graham Price some time later he told me I was still a Lion and should wear the regalia. But when I asked him to reverse roles to see what he would have done, he had to admit that he wouldn't have considered himself a Lion either. There is no doubt about it, if you don't play it doesn't count.

Anyway, I may not have been a Lion on my own terms but I could still look back over a remarkable twelve months. As a player you are lucky if a season such as that appears once in your lifetime and it wasn't long before the magic started to fade. When the 1980-81 season got under way Lancashire seemed set for a repeat performance in the county championship, but Northumberland determination saw us toppled from our pedestal at Gosforth stadium. The game was a dreadful stop-start affair and I suspect that it was possibly the final straw for Tony Neary because he announced his retirement from the game shortly afterwards; Roger Uttley wasn't far behind.

That left England without two key men from the Grand Slam team for the opening championship match against Wales in Cardiff but it was still a confident squad that journeyed down to the Principality. We were, after all, the reigning champions. David Cooke, of Harlequins, took over from Nero and Mike Rafter was picked out of position at blind side. That latter decision proved to be a bad one in the sense that Mike couldn't compete with

Jeff Squire at 5 in the lineout and the Welshman won a lot of ball in an area we had hoped to dominate.

The game was only seventeen minutes old when our third world-class forward departed. Soon after the start Fran made a dash for the corner and might well have scored had he not pulled a hamstring. He tried to battle on but eventually had to limp off, head bowed, and I had a funny feeling he might be walking from a rugby field for the last time. I think the crowd sensed something too because they gave him a very warm reception as he left the field without achieving his one remaining ambition, to beat the Welsh in their own backyard.

We didn't play particularly well but Paul Dodge made a marvellous break to send Dusty Hare in for a great try and we were leading by a point as the game moved into injury time. I was beginning to think that Fran might at least have been part of a historic victory on Welsh soil when the referee caught Clive Woodward offside in our own 25. He had been caught when Brynmor Williams pulled one of the oldest tricks in a scrum half's repertoire by feinting to pick the ball out of the back row of a scrum.

Poor Woody was inconsolable and Steve Fenwick kicked the goal to win the game for Wales. Dusty had one last chance to tip the balance the other way, as he had at Twickenham the year before, but he didn't quite make it. On that occasion it was little comfort knowing that I had got away with my boob in the Grand Slam run-in.

Meanwhile, Fran had gone straight to the hotel, and when I saw his wife, Pat, she told me his temperature had soared and she had had to call a doctor. He had had the problem before and when we got back to Manchester a skin complaint was diagnosed and an appointment made with a specialist. He confirmed a condition which meant that his temperature would flare up if he got dirt in even the smallest cut. For an international forward cuts are impossible to avoid so, in fairness to his family, who had already had to live through the traumas of South Africa the previous summer, he decided to call it a day.

Only Billy and Wheelbrace remained of my long-standing chums in the pack and a period of real change was setting in. For the next game against Scotland at Twickenham the selectors brought in Nick Jeavons in place of Mike Rafter at blind side and Colin Smart took over from Fran in the front row. Johnny Horton had pulled a hamstring so Huw Davies stepped in at fly half for what turned out to be an enjoyable, high-scoring game which we won 23–17 with Huw scoring a great debut try.

We went over to Dublin with a 50 per cent record and that was a great game. We lost Phil Blakeway and Gordon Sargent came on, with Smarty switching to tight-head. The first scrum after that went back about six yards in the direction of our line and I thought we were in for a torrid time. The days of panic were a thing of the past, however, the lads responded really well to this challenge and we eventually ran out 10–6 winners to set the stage for the final game against an unbeaten French side.

The game was shrouded in controversy because of a decision by Billy and another by referee Alan Hosie. Bill's decision, after winning the toss, was to play into the strong wind and he was heavily criticized for it afterwards. But all the lads had agreed with him as they wanted to play into the wind first, to get it out of the way. We started well too and but for a blatantly illegal try we might have won. That's where Mr Hosie comes in. The ball went into the stand – into the lap of Dickie Jeeps to be precise – and France took a quick throw with another ball tossed to them by a ball boy, galloped away and scored a try. We couldn't believe it when Mr Hosie allowed the score to stand.

We really tore into the French in the second half but they held on to win and we had to settle for second place in the championship. Still, after so many years at the other end of the table it was a reasonable season.

When summer came around we went on tour to Argentina and that proved to be a cock-up from day one.

It was the middle of winter there and we were put straight into a country club that didn't have any heating. The beds were damp and we saw a beetle that was so huge we seriously considered putting Johnny Horton on it and having a bit of a race. Thankfully, we only stayed one night and that was one occasion when it wasn't entirely the fault of our Argentinian hosts. They had wanted to put us up in a hotel in the first place but it transpired some old RFU official had stayed at the country club soon after the war and insisted on the team staying there.

After one extremely uncomfortable night we were moved into the Sheraton in the centre of Buenos Aires and that was much more to our taste, even if we found our daily allowance to be something of a farce. We each received £5 a day but a bottle of beer cost £4. If you wanted to go into a nightclub you had to be ready to part with £20 to cover the entrance fee, and tennis was a real racket at £100 a session. Needless to say we played little tennis, drank less beer than is good for a tourist and couldn't even charge for coffee in our rooms. If we went out of the hotel all we could afford to do was walk.

The only activities we were able to get involved in were those that had been organized for us. With Rugby Union on a social par with polo out there, the activities weren't terribly to our taste. They tended to be men-only affairs, usually old-fashioned dinners that seemed to drag on for ever with half an hour between courses and long, boring speeches. Our one salvation was tour manager Derek Morgan. With his Welsh connections the lads were a bit unsure of him at first but he turned up trumps by fighting for a better deal for his players. He even sorted out the coffee situation, which was marvellous for me because I'm a bit of a coffee-olic when I'm staying in hotels.

Weekends tended to be spent at the Sheraton, which was a nice break, but during the week we would be taken out to play in one-horse towns where the horse had been shot.

The impression we all came away with was that the Argentinians were totally incapable of organizing anything and when the Falklands War broke out later I was quite confident it would be no contest. If they took us to a golf club there would be no clubs to play with. If we were driven off to play tennis there would be no rackets. They also had a strange idea of cultural visits. I remember the first really warm and sunny day, with the mercury touching the low eighties and the lads relaxing around the hotel pool for the first time. We were unwinding nicely when we were told to don our 'number ones' and pile aboard a coach. For the next hour and a half we melted in that coach only to discover the object of our journey was to look at a dam. I think they had envisaged a guided tour but we took one look at the mass of concrete, turned round and drove all the way back to town again. I can tell you, that dam didn't half get some stick. They're lucky we didn't blow it up.

That same evening we were taken out to sample a local culinary delicacy and our tongues were hanging out as we waited two hours for it to be prepared. When it arrived it looked as though they had simply dipped a bucket into the ocean. There was everything imaginable floating around and none of us could eat it.

In spite of our problems the spirit amongst the lads was very high and without the normal disco and party scene we set about making our own entertainment. Clint Magregor was one of the props and he used to treat us to Jamaican songs – a sort of butchered version of Harry Belafonte – and Mike Rafter, who actually has a very good voice, led us through the full range of West Country numbers.

The games we played were hard. I don't quite know what our ancestors did but it seems that wherever we go in the world everyone wants to beat hell out of us. Nigel Melville was on that tour and played well, so I had to do likewise to keep the young rascal out of the team.

We discovered that the Argentinians' forte was scrummaging and we struggled to hold them in the first Test. It looked unpromising until the last minute when Clive Woodward levelled the score with a try under the posts and we converted it to win. The crowd went mad, whistling their heads off, blowing trumpets and setting off fire crackers. As the opposition trooped off the pitch, looking thoroughly dejected, I said to Mike Davis that we had them then. Sure enough, we won the remaining Test rather more comfortably. But a great cheer went up from the lads when our aircraft started to lift off the tarmac, homeward bound.

Just before the start of the following season, 1981–82, Lancashire went on tour to the South of France. As I had already taken more than my share of time off work that year, I flew out later with Billy Beaumont and John Carleton to play in the game against Béziers, where Bill's troubles really began. It was a terrific game, terribly hard, which Béziers won with a drop goal ten minutes into injury time. Had they not dropped that goal when they did we would probably still have been playing.

After we had scored what looked like the winning try late in the second half, the French kicked off, ignored the ball completely and smashed straight into Billy. It was a cold, cynical act and Bill was in a terrible state. He was groggy for a very long time and that's when some people started to look into his medical history – possibly prompted by a remark made by a French doctor to the effect that if the X-rays had been his own son's he would never have let him play the game again. Word soon started to filter through English rugby circles on our return about the risk Bill could be taking, but he seemed to recover completely, led Lancashire successfully on the county championship trail and unsuccessfully against Australia, who were touring Britain and had been given a game against the Red Rose county.

England's meeting with the Wallabies will best be remembered as the Erica Roe game. That's the occasion when she of the substantial mammaries ran half naked on to the pitch at half time while we players tried to suck our oranges and look serious. At the time, Bill had

141

gathered us around him with his back to the action, and was giving us a bit of earache about our first-half performance which hadn't been particularly auspicious. When Erica ran on with a similarly unclad companion, we started grinning and Bill, who wasn't prepared to look round, couldn't understand how he had completely lost our attention. Then Peter Wheeler, who couldn't contain himself any longer, chipped in with, 'Hey Bill, a bloke's just run on with your arse on his chest.'

That little offering from Wheelbrace really destroyed us because we were always poking fun at Bill's oddly shaped backside. It was my practice at squad sessions to pat it as I walked past and inquire as to how his outboard motor was that day.

The interlude must have acted as a tonic because we played much better in the second half and won the game comfortably. Perhaps the Aussies were too busy thinking about big-breasted sheilas; I believe Erica, who received enormous publicity to match her physical attributes, joined our overseas visitors for a few days. Actually, I felt sorry for her pal because she got no publicity and I've always contended that she had the better body anyway.

Frivolity over, it was back to the international championship against Scotland at Murrayfield where we didn't see so much as a raised kilt. A quiet drama was enacted before that game because, unknown to most people, Bill was taken ill on the Friday night and a doctor had to be called. He recovered sufficiently to play the following day, but as we made our way to the ground he told me that I would have been captain if he had had to pull out of the game. That was the first indication I had ever had that I might one day captain England. I had always assumed that in the event of something happening to Bill, Wheelbrace would have been asked to take the reins.

I thought we might have won the Triple Crown that season but Andy Irvine foiled us yet again and we had to settle for a draw. After that it was off to Moseley to play North Midlands in the county championship final. Little did we realize what drama was to unfold.

Before the game, Lancashire were regarded as hot favourites but North Midlands skipper, Les Cusworth, had organized his troops very well and we had to fight all the way. They played particularly well during the first half hour with John Davidson completely dominating the lineout.

Billy took a knock early on and it was soon obvious to me that he was in trouble. He confirmed that when he asked me not to throw the ball to him at lineouts. I told him he ought to go off. He wouldn't, of course, so I told him he was being stupid, didn't know what was going on and was playing badly. In spite of my concerned advice he stayed on; I suspect he had the sense to realize that if he went off it might be for the last time. During a stoppage I managed to convey a message to Des Seabrook, our coach, and he got the team doctor, Noel Atkinson, on to have a look at him. Big, brave Bill was still reluctant to go and the pair of them almost had to drag him off the pitch and into a dressing room.

Dave Cusani, the tall Orrell lock, came on as replacement and immediately increased our options by winning lineout ball. We started to play like champions at last and Tony Wright slipped over for the winning try. North Midlands had proved a far stronger side than they had been given the credit for being, but our delight at beating them was somewhat muted that evening. Those of us who had travelled the world with Bill and were close friends knew we had possibly played our last game with the great man.

Bill cried off the Irish match at Twickenham the following week and that led to a lot of speculation as to who would captain England in his absence. I had been told by Bill that the job would be given to me, but, knowing selectors as I did, I couldn't be sure. Speculation was rife in the press, with some pundits clearly favouring Wheelbrace and others going for me. I started to feel the pressure because the telephone never stopped ringing and it was impossible to get off the sports pages.

On the Monday I was busy decorating a new house I had just bought and became so engrossed (something that doesn't normally happen with me in the domestic chores department) that I missed my lift to the England squad session at Stourbridge. When I arrived somewhat late, Budge called me to one side and I suspected a rollicking. Instead he asked me to captain my country.

The lads all responded well, but on the day of the match my team talk was an absolute shambles. I was so emotionally involved that I lost my thread completely and it reminded me of my inane ramblings when I captained Cheshire at the age of eighteen. My eyes blazed passion, I was thumping the table with my fists and ranting on about history and our great English heritage. Even the IRA got a mention and the result was that we all ran on to the pitch and played like bloody headless chickens. We were awful and it was all my fault.

What a shambles of a weekend, but Ireland played very well and, although I was desperately disappointed that we lost, I was genuinely pleased for the Irish lads and told them so at the dinner afterwards. They had lost every single game the previous season but never by more than 4 points. The selectors had virtually kept faith with the same players throughout at a time when selectors in other countries would have been chopping and changing in desperation. Quite apart from which, the Irish lads are a great bunch, their attitude is absolutely right and when they win they don't force the fact down your throat all night.

After that weekend the whole world caved in. Bill and I were on the telephone round the clock and we did an awful lot of soul-searching. He didn't know what to do about his future and I told him not to put himself under pressure in that way. The only thing he could do was to place himself in the hands of the medical experts and leave them to make the decisions. That's exactly what happened and it was for the best. For the sake of another couple of seasons at the top and a few more caps it wasn't worth risking further beatings, and the way he played the game inevitably put him at risk. There is nobody more delighted than I am that he has made such a success of retirement.

When England broke the news of Bill's retirement I made sure I was hidden away in Wales on business. I knew Wheelbrace was being strongly pushed for the captaincy but I felt there was a personal thing between him and Budge that would prevent him getting the job. Had John Scott not been injured the previous season he might well have got it, because he was always Budge's favourite, but the honour landed in my lap like a hot potato.

I always felt that the selectors were going to push Nigel Melville into the side at any time and I realized Paris wasn't the best place to take a team that had just had its heart ripped out. My folks were upset about all the press talk but I told them not to be and also to be ready for the French game being my last international. I knew deep down that another poor performance in Paris would almost certainly seal my fate.

So, if this was to be my shoot-out at the O K Corral, I decided my pistols had better be loaded. When I arrived at Stourbridge for the squad session I put all my cards on the table, telling them that I had been given the job and if I was to succeed I had to have them solidly behind me, as they had been with Bill. The reaction was marvellous; it was typical of Peter Wheeler that he had already telephoned me when the side was announced and told me to forget the rubbish I was reading in the newspapers He said that he, for one, was right behind me.

From that moment I knew I had their confidence and my team talk in Paris was considerably better than the one I had delivered at Twickenham. The real problem for an international skipper is not firing the players up but calming them down and getting across exactly what you expect of them out on the park. It's quite a harrowing experience but I worked very well with Mike Davis, whom I had grown to respect, and we had a couple of very good training sessions. In the Irish game the ball had been getting stuck in the front two rows at the scrums and Scotty had had the criticism unfairly heaped at his door. We sorted that problem out at the sessions and on the day we won deservedly.

Everything went just as we had planned, including a try that Clive Woodward scored after a long dropout by Mike Slemen. A lot of people thought that was a spur-of-the-moment act by Mike but it wasn't. It was a move we had rehearsed a number of times.

I had plenty to celebrate that evening, having led England to victory and equalled Dickie Jeeps's record number of caps for a scrum half. The champagne flowed but it wasn't a strong enough brew for one member of the side. That was the occasion when aftershave came into its own as an aperitif and Colin Smart speaks highly of its intoxicating qualities. The one problem with the French game is that everything is dragged out and it is very late before you actually get anything to eat – remembering, of course, that some lads don't eat at all before a match. Without food, but with wine and beer readily available, it's little wonder that the lads start to get boisterous and fuel is added to the fire by putting all the players at the same table.

That evening I was sitting on the top table and could see things warming up a little. What I didn't know was that Maurice Colclough had conned Smarty. The French always leave gifts for each guest at the dinner and that year the crop of goodies included a bottle of aftershave. Big Maurice quietly poured the contents out of his bottle and filled it with wine, which he proceeded to drink, daring Smarty (who wasn't on that occasion) to drink his. He obliged, ended up in hospital and the press gang had something to write about. Poor old Colin couldn't believe the fuss when he arrived back home, stomach recovered but smelling like a puff!

Once the dust had settled and people stopped thrusting bottles of aftershave in front of us at dinners, we got down to the serious business of confronting Wales at Twickenham. We won and I became the most capped scrum half in English rugby. Added to that, confidence was high, we seemed to have patched over the loss of four world-class forwards and, with a tour to Canada and America looming up, the future looked decidedly rosy.

10

'Wine to Water' (1982–83)

England's very successful tour of Canada and America during the summer of 1982 should have set us up for the following season, although, with hindsight, the level of the opposition might have given us a slightly false impression of our strength. And then there was the unsettling period caused by the Adidas boot scandal.

That little episode stemmed directly from references to boot money in Mickey Burton's controversial autobiography* and the tax man decided that it was an area worthy of investigation. What a lot of people didn't realize was that Rugby Union was only a part of it and people in many other sports suddenly found themselves having to declare large sums of money to the Inland Revenue. Rugby Union cash, by all accounts, was peanuts in comparison. Lads from other sports were all asking the same question: 'Who the bloody hell is Mickey Burton and where do I lay my hands on him?'

Controversial to the last, that was Mickey, and he certainly stirred up a hornets' nest, although it has to be said that not all senior Rugby Union players were involved. Those who were fell into a 'privileged' category so far as the sports companies were concerned. It was therefore wrong for anyone to assume that everyone who pulled on an international jersey was guilty of taking backhanders.

Adidas, of course, came in for an enormous amount of criticism, particularly from the RFU, but that was wrong because all the sports gear companies were at it.

*Mickey Burton, *Never Stay Down* (Queen Anne Press, 1982)

Payments had clearly got out of hand anyway and I think the rival companies were trying to outbid each other for players' services. It is quite likely that in the end the companies themselves were being exploited, but they were benefiting in a number of ways. They certainly had a cheap form of advertising, bearing in mind the prime advertising time they obtained and the small sums of money I heard being bandied about.

I think the man who came out of the whole lamentable business on the credit side was Robin Money, the former Leicester and Wilmslow player, who is the Adidas representative. When the taxman arrived to go through the company books he felt it only fair to let people know what was happening and tell them they would be taxed on income received from the company. He sent out letters to each individual sportsman informing him of payments he had received during a period of two to three years. That action allowed those involved to enter the amounts on their tax forms to avoid prosecution by the Inland Revenue. To the best of my knowledge, Adidas was the only company to take that action yet they caught the full wrath of the RFU.

There was a backlash effect on the England team because the whole thing was very unsettling, but the saga did have its lighter moments. It was very difficult motivating the lads for the first international of the season against a Fijian side that was touring the country but not making any sort of impression. The mood in our camp was good, but lighthearted, and just as I was trying to switch them on to the task ahead during the team talk, in waltzed RFU secretary, Bob Weighill, with an armful of black marker pens. He then proceeded to instruct us on how to black out the distinctive stripes on our Adidas boots. That caused great amusement and, like children in a classroom, the lads started marking one another. By the time they had finished they looked blacker than the Fijians. Amidst all that joviality there was no point whatsoever in trying to deliver a serious team talk until we were actually in the dressing room at

Twickenham.

Wherever you went at that time there was an under-current suggestion that you had become a professional person and gibes came from people both inside and outside the game. That was very disruptive and the one bloke who really suffered was Peter Wheeler. It was thought in rugby's corridors of power that Wheelbrace was some sort of shop steward acting on behalf of the players in money deals with Adidas and I honestly believe that went against him in Lions selection later, especially so far as the captaincy was concerned. People at the top had a totally wrong impression of Peter and put an unfair slant on his character.

With blacked-out boots and characters, the Fijian game came and went, the lads playing really well to coast to a comfortable victory. To their credit the Fijians hit back late in the game with two beautiful tries that proved to be real crowd pleasers. Having visited Fiji some years earlier I knew how much the islanders enjoy certain aspects of our game but they don't really want to know about scrums, lineouts, rucks and mauls. All they want is to be able to run and handle – great to watch, but it's a naïve concept that simply doesn't work against British sides. Mind you, I've heard since that they are adjusting their technique and if ever they get their tight play right the Fijians will be a force to be reckoned with.

After the Fijian match things seemed to go relatively smoothly, but the Adidas business was still hovering in the background and injuries to Clive Woodward and Nick Jeavons didn't give me peace of mind. I felt Mike Slemen had been wrongly chopped from the side and I was very concerned when Phil Blakeway announced his retirement from the game. Suddenly we were without four top-class performers and they were disruptions we could ill afford.

So, things weren't going quite as smoothly as many people thought, even though the final trial seemed to indicate that the machine was still ticking over nicely. The selectors came up with two strong sides on paper and I expected a close game. Instead, we swamped the opposition and the way the lads performed that afternoon, albeit in an unreal situation, started me thinking that in spite of my foreboding we could have something special going for us.

We opened our campaign against France at Twickenham and I waited for the announcement of the French team with bated breath because they are the most difficult side to beat when their fickle selectors get it right. When I saw the team list I knew they had got it absolutely right and it was obviously going to be a very trying afternoon.

The front row of Paparemborde, Dintrans and Dospital needed no introduction to us and the back row looked as strong as usual. I didn't know much about the second row of Orso and Condom, but Maurice Colclough told me they were both big, young and aggressive players who would be as keen as mustard to do well at Twickenham. They proved to be just that and I heard a nice story later of how Condom had played for the Irish Wolfhounds in a game at Broughton Park and had been introduced, tongue in cheek, to a young lady of Irish descent called Coyle. That sounds like a pretty safe relationship!

So, the pack was obviously going to be a tough unit to dominate and the only time I have ever played on a winning side against France was when we succeeded in outscrummaging them. It is essential you do that so you can tie in their back row, in much the same way you need to do with the All Blacks. Then you tell your big men to run at their small men and that is a tactic the French don't enjoy very much.

For this particular game I wasn't too pleased to discover that all their backs, with the exception of the scrum half, were under-10-second sprinters over 100 yards.

A difficult game was in prospect and we lost the mainstay of our pack in the first half when big Maurice had to go off with an injury that kept him out of action

151

until the British Lions tour that summer. His replacement, Bob Hesford, played well, but he couldn't totally take over the role of a player as important to the side as Maurice was. From being red-hot favourites, one or two little things turned everything round and we were in a very different ball game, which we lost 15–19. Even so, the lads reacted well and I had a long chat with Budge about things when he came to my room at the hotel later. We talked our way through the game, trying to analyse what went wrong and I felt at the time that we had really understood each other. Our belief that we had been beaten by a good side was borne out later when France shared the title with Ireland.

The selectors didn't panic and brought in Steve Boyle to replace Maurice at lock for the Welsh game. Peter Wheeler dropped out and Steve Mills, another man of Gloucester, took his place in the front row. I had been on a couple of tours with Millsey so had no qualms about his selection. He had always been a very sound performer and I knew he would do a good job for us, so the England party moved off to Cardiff in confident mood. Ringing in our ears were suggestions that we were in line for the Triple Crown while the demise of Welsh rugby was nigh.

I did a lot of groundwork before the game and called John Carleton, John Scott and Colin Smart to a summit conference in my room at the hotel. This had to be a real death-or-glory job, I told them, as this was a game when the future of certain players could be on the line. Therefore we really needed to get our act together and, as the senior players in the team, I wanted their help.

The three of them responded magnificently, especially Smarty, whom I had never seen so wound up. He actually smacked a guy in training and for Colin to show that kind of aggression was just what I wanted. Of course, playing all his rugby in Wales, this was a very big match for him, especially as he was going out to play against his old adversary, Graham Price.

There is always a big build-up to the game at the Arms

Park and I remember sitting the lads down in the dressing room and trying to remind them how they would have felt as young schoolboys if they realized that in eighty minutes they could change history and record the first English win in Cardiff since 1963. This was to be their chance to do just that and they responded well to the challenge. By the time they reached the pitch they were really fired up and played magnificent rugby for the first twenty minutes. Perhaps we played too well during that period, releasing too much ammunition too soon and leaving both players and spectators believing we might not merely beat Wales but enjoy something of a landslide victory against them for a change.

We scored a good try through John Carleton and Steve Bainbridge won a steady stream of lineout possession until Bob Norster moved from 2 to 4 to mark him. With the help of Jeff Squire that source dried up and that was one of the reasons less options were open to us in the second half. There was also a period when there was a series of scrums with the Welsh put-in and that again limited our possession. After the match we were criticized for changing our tactics and starting to play a tighter game, which was simply not true. Our tactics never varied once during the game. Our intention from the start had been to get deep into Welsh territory and then attack them by running at people. But, as the game progressed, we couldn't do it without the ball.

The real sickener came when Wales scored the most ridiculous try I have ever been involved in. The ball was tapped back at a lineout close to our line and I went to set up a ruck by pushing the ball back between my legs. Jeff Squire, who suddenly dived over the top, found the ball in his arms on our side of the ruck and all he had to do was pop it down over the line. I was filled with disbelief when the referee awarded a try and Jeff, who is an old pal of mine, looked at me, winked and went off laughing back to the halfway line. That put us behind, but good old Dusty Hare performed his customary Andy Irvine style rescue act to earn us the draw (13–13) that was the very least we deserved.

Off the field the atmosphere in the rival camps was totally different. I wandered into the Welsh dressing room to thank them for the game and found them totally despondent. They knew they had been well beaten but had escaped with a draw; the misery was explained to me later by Graham Price who said they had never considered the possibility of losing and hadn't believed we were even capable of giving them a game. Meanwhile, the England lads were quite jubilant. They realized they could, and should, have won, but they had achieved the best English result in Cardiff for twenty years and felt they could go on to perform great feats in the two remaining championship games.

I had injured my ribs during the game and was sprawled on the treatment table with a pack of ice on the tender area when Budge walked in. I could tell by his face that he wasn't very happy. As the lads were feeling reasonably pleased with themselves I didn't want him to spoil the mood at that stage – I've always felt the next squad session is the time for full inquests – so I grabbed hold of him and asked him to look calm, keep his chin up and not show the lads he was feeling down. I suggested he and I could have a long chat back at the hotel, as we had had after the French game, but he wasn't really listening and stormed off. Perhaps I should have been more suspicious when he returned later, placed an arm round my shoulder, father fashion, and said that because of my injury I should take my time, stay with the lads and leave him to handle the usual post-match press conference.

As the injury was quite painful I thanked him, little knowing that at the conference he would tell all and sundry that the blame for England's failure lay with the halfbacks. I felt later it was a knife in the back, but at the time I was totally unaware of it and went off to the dinner in a happy frame of mind.

The press boys aren't slow to latch on to that sort of comment, however, and I couldn't believe my eyes when

I started reading the newspapers the following morning. It had been a very big game for the players. They had drawn with Wales, while I had been involved in a personal battle with one of the world's greatest scrum halves and had come through the test well. As it was a Lions year there was no way I was going to let Terry Holmes get the better of me. By the time I got back home my family and friends, who had all seen the game on television, were amazed by the stories that were coming out of Cardiff. I have news for them. So was I.

By making those comments, Budge had ensured good copy for the media for several days because it had become obvious the captain was about to get the chop. When that happens it's big news, but not much fun when you are on the receiving end of it.

The prediction came true. I was in my office on the following Monday morning when Budge made a 10p call from a coin box to tell me I had been dropped for the game against Scotland at Twickenham.

I just said, 'OK, it's your decision. I'll see you at the squad session. I presume I'm on the bench?'

He said I wasn't. Nigel Melville would be in the side, Nick Youngs would be replacement and it would be rather embarrassing to have me there. John Scott would be captain.

A few minutes later I got a call from Don Rutherford at HQ, checking to see if Budge had actually called me. I understood that he hadn't really wanted to and that Don was making sure he had. And there was me thinking Budge had done the decent thing spontaneously without having to be forced into it. As the days went by I came to realize how kind some people can be. I received a lot of letters of sympathy from members of the public and people in the game and I soon got over my disappointment. After all, I might have lost the captaincy and a place in the side, but I had memories that nobody could take away.

That, I said to myself, is it. With all my experience, though, I should have known better than that as an ironic card of fate had still to be played. I was quite enjoying myself in the early hours in a Manchester night spot when there was a telephone call for me from a newspaper reporter. It turned out to be Andy Sokill, my old rugby-playing pal from schooldays, who writes for the *Daily Express*. He told me that Nigel had limped off in training and was in a bad way. In all probability, he said, they were going to call me back into the side.

However, as Nick had already been named as Nigel's replacement, I couldn't see the selectors jumping me over him. So I decided to ignore the rumours and got on with things as usual, until Budge called to say they wanted me to play.

When I arrived at the training ground on the Thursday before the game I was embarrassed, my pal Scotty was embarrassed (he'd been the first on the phone to me after I had been dropped) and the selectors were embarrassed. Matters were made worse when I was asked to play the sort of game they had clearly expected from Nigel; they didn't want to change the strategy they had hoped to adopt for the game. It was to be a complete change of style from the one we had used in recent seasons and I couldn't see the sense in shovelling the ball out all the time against a side like Scotland. The way to play the Scots is to give them a hard time in the front five, attack them close in and tie in the back row. As they were playing a back-row forward, Iain Paxton, at lock, those tactics seemed even more appropriate.

I went out and moved the ball as I had been told to, even though it was against my better judgement. But at the back of my mind was all the talk after the Welsh game that we should have kept spinning the ball out to the marvellous English backs to enable them to run in try after try. If you keep hearing things like that you start wondering if you are wrong and perhaps those advocating change are right. Anyway, I gave their game a try and it played totally into the hands of the Scots, who won handsomely, 22–12. It must have been the only international I ever played in where I never kicked the ball and although some might suggest I should have changed the tactics in mid-stream, it's worth recalling that I would have been going back to tactics that had led to my being dropped in the first place.

England's season was in tatters after that game; it was all so unnecessary. It was like being back in the seventies and morale had returned to that all-time low. When the selectors announced the side to play Ireland in Dublin Nick had been elevated and I was back on the bench. From being captain I had been dropped twice within the space of four weeks.

The next act in the drama came when the side was announced to the press and Geoff Green, who writes on rugby for the *Manchester Evening News*, telephoned to see if I wanted to comment on being dropped again. I told him I preferred to say nothing and left it at that.

A few minutes later I heard that one national newspaper had an article in which Budge was reported to have commented 'scathingly' that I had tried to play like Nigel. It was claimed later that the comment had been 'off the record', but that didn't help me because it was in print. I went to have a chat with Fran Cotton, whose office is next to mine, and his reaction was that I should give Budge 'what for'.

I told him I wasn't too keen to do that because, having just been dropped, people would say I was merely having a whinge (which is what one not totally unexpected columnist suggested later). But the more I thought about it, the angrier I became. If it was wrong for me to have a moan it must also be wrong for selectors to make derogatory comments about players. We are, when all is said and done, amateur players, living and playing under a lot of pressure, who go onto the field to do our best. The matter debated, I picked up the telephone, rang Geoff and gave him my two pennyworth. I said selectors were wrong to comment publicly about individual players and suggested that they destroyed team morale by axing players after the Welsh game.

When the story broke I had the whole world ringing

up, but, apart from Geoff, I deliberately only spoke to one of the other Manchester press lads whom I trusted, Cammie Stewart of the *Daily Express*, and sat back waiting for the flak. My little outburst made headline news and that was bound to be interesting because I was still a member of the England squad.

I travelled to Stourbridge for the training session before the Dublin game and walked in with a scarf wrapped firmly over my mouth – a little piece of light relief that brought the house down with the lads, although I don't think Budge was too pleased about it. He lectured us about irresponsible chatter to the press, which I thought was quite amusing considering that that was the sole reason for my outburst. Reaction from players made it clear that they felt it was time somebody stood up and said something.

Off we went to Ireland, but, with the home side in for a share of the title, it was a no-hope situation. Last-minute dramas seemed to be the order of the day and Scotty was taken ill on the Friday. That's when a chink of sanity shone through because Peter Wheeler was asked to take over if John didn't recover in time.

With the captain on his sick bed the next drama revolved around which wing David Trick should play on, having been brought into the side. As John Carleton was already established as one of the best right wings in the world the question should never have arisen. Whoever stepped in had to be prepared to play on the left wing because moving John would have been ridiculous. With a Lions tour looming, J.C. was understandably reluctant to switch berths.

It was a shambles of a couple of days, but Scotty recovered sufficiently to lead the side and at the end of the day we got away lightly. The final score of 25–15 to Ireland was no testimony to the preparation and selection of the England team because respectability was provided by Dusty, who kicked everything in sight.

Two days later the British Lions party to tour New Zealand was announced and the England players had been largely overlooked. I felt terribly sorry for Peter Wheeler, who would have made the ideal captain, quite apart from his vast experience and reputation as the world's best hooker. There was nobody more delighted than myself when Derek Morgan took over as chairman of the England selectors and made Peter captain, an honour that was long overdue.

At the end of the campaign I had a very interesting chat with Mike Davis, who, as coach, produced the classic line that he had 'turned wine into water'. I don't think he should take the blame for that because he had found himself in an unenviable position during that last season. He had announced at the start that he would relinquish the post at the end of term, but he was a schoolteacher, not a politician, and couldn't understand why people who had previously voted with him suddenly started to vote against him in selection. He wasn't a sufficiently political animal to see that allegiances would switch in the belief that Budge would stay on as chairman.

Mike found himself being outvoted on crucial issues, the first being the decision to drop Mike Slemen. He had also been against rocking the boat after the Welsh game, but the vote went against him and we all finished up in the sea. The Adidas business hadn't helped either and I gather that at one stage the selectors had considered dropping Wheelbrace from the squad altogether, which would have been ridiculous.

The more I think back to the Welsh game, the more I think people got it out of context. It was the first game Wales had played that season and some people thought they were going to be a pushover, hence the reaction when we didn't push them over but drew with them instead. The harsh truth is that no Welsh side, however poor, is a pushover against England at Cardiff, and it is worth remembering that the only game they lost that season was against France in Paris.

The selectors should have kept their nerve after the Welsh game as Mike apparently wanted them to. But doubts were being cast over his ability as a coach and that was equally ridiculous. He coached the Grand Slam side, never lost a game on the tours to the Far East, Argentina, Canada and America, and generally did a good job, earning the friendship and respect of his players. It's rather sad the way things turned sour. The president that season, J. V. Smith, never seemed to be out of the newspapers breathing fire and brimstone. He criticized the South Africans but turned up for the Five Nations tournament there, and he simply wouldn't let the Adidas issue die. So far as the selectors were concerned, they abandoned the continuity they had established and dismantled the good platform set up during the three previous years.

It was inevitable that the disquiet would filter through to the players and the team played with less and less confidence, losing belief in their collective and individual abilities and finishing up holding the all too familiar wooden spoon. It really was a case of turning wine into water, but don't blame yourself, Mike.

11

From Lion Cub to Captain (1983–84)

Whenever a British Lions tour leaves these shores a good many players are left behind clutching reserve cards. Also left behind are players who have received a special letter telling them they are on immediate stand-by, with the instruction to keep themselves especially fit. What that means, in effect, is that you are the player called out in the event of an injury in your own specialist position.

After the sort of season I had just had I was rather surprised to get such a letter because I had had the feeling I was right out of the picture. So, as someone was bound to get injured, I decided to look upon the possibility of a trip to New Zealand as a bonus and John Lawrence, the nice guy who acts as secretary to the Four Home Unions, expressed his own delight for me, bearing in mind that I had travelled all the way to South Africa during the previous tour just to keep the replacements' bench warm. Having just returned from Bermuda again, all the doom and gloom started to lift and I was able seriously to cherish the thought that I might, after all, play just one game for the British Lions to enable me to die happy!

Things never seem to run smoothly for me in international rugby and what turned out to be a fateful day started very early when I got up to watch the first Test against New Zealand on television. When Terry Holmes got injured and had to leave the field looking in a pretty bad way, the telephone started to ring. The entire world seemed to be calling to check if I was on my way to New Zealand. I had to tell them I hadn't heard anything but might have a chance if they would all get off the bloody line.

I switched the television set to Ceefax and the message there was to the effect that I was the likely replacement for Terry. But the hours ticked by and, although the telephone was red hot, there was no call that really mattered. I even received two calls from newspapers in New Zealand and that made me think I would be on my travels again. With that thought foremost in my mind I took myself out on to the park at the rear of my house and subjected the anatomy to a really stiff session. No messages had arrived by the time I got back, but I switched on 'Grandstand' just in time to hear Gareth Edwards repeat the earlier belief that I was the likely replacement. That provided an added spur and I dashed off to a sports club in the centre of Manchester for a real sweat session, having already taken the precaution of crying off a cricket match I had been due to play that afternoon for my local club, Brooklands.

Two journalists turned up at the club where I was training, having diligently tracked me down, to take pictures, and when people wanted to know why I was the centre of such attention I had to tell them it appeared I 'might' be going to New Zealand.

By the time I got back to base I was getting more than a little worried because there was still no message and all the old doubts had started creeping in. I returned to Ceefax and there it was in black and white. Nigel Melville had been called up instead. I thought I had grown accustomed to disappointment, but that was a shattering blow and I was very upset. People kept ringing to ask how I felt – silly question – and I muttered things to the effect that I was a bit downhearted but not totally surprised. The only problem was that when the newspapers came out the following day they read rather as though I was whingeing. I wasn't. Nor was I getting at Nigel, because he's a great lad and a lovely footballer, who has had his own share of misfortune too. It was a year when I just couldn't stay out of the headlines, no

162

matter how hard I tried.

At that point I said to myself, 'That's it. That really is it.'

The hard, daily grind of training stopped and I kept fit merely by playing squash and cricket regularly. I was quite clearly never, ever, going to become a British Lion and decided all I could do was get used to the idea and pursue other goals, or pleasures.

Time is a great healer and I started to adjust to that idea. Life was still sociable enough and I crashed into bed in the early hours of one morning only to be disturbed by the bedside telephone ringing at about seven a.m. Whoever it was obviously knew little about my sleeping habits and I simply ignored the noisy intrusion, turned over and was soon back in the land of nod. When it rang again an hour later I decided to answer simply to stop it ringing. It was John Lawrence on the other end of the line and he announced himself as 'the shit'. That was because he had been clearly embarrassed by the previous occasion when Nigel had been called up instead of me. Now, Nigel was injured and I was required after all.

John said he was delighted for me, but I wanted to know why he hadn't bothered to ring me when Terry got himself injured, in order to put me out of my misery and at least enable me to escape an endlessly ringing telephone. I didn't press the point but suspect he had been advised against making a call on that occasion.

Having invited me to journey to the other side of the world, John then requested my presence in London for a fitness test. Apparently I was required to run a mile, a quick 400 metres, a series of sprints and go through an assortment of exercises, all within half an hour. Being an old campaigner, my reaction was very different from what one would expect from a young player being given the opportunity of a lifetime. I told John I didn't fancy doing that and he insisted I had to. I then suggested I did it by myself in my own back garden, but he said I would have to be seen doing it. In response to that I said I was definitely not leaping on a plane there and then

163

and dashing to London to prove I was fit enough to do things I knew I could do anyway. I also said I was due to play cricket that afternoon and wasn't backing out a second time.

As a parting shot I said that even if I failed the fitness test there weren't any scrum halves left in Britain to send out. John finally gave in and I went off to play my beloved cricket.

I opened the innings against Bowdon and in the very first over their pace bowler rapped me on the wrist with a quickly rising delivery. My hand went numb and I won't tell you what I was thinking. A scrum half with a broken wrist is about as much use as a footballer with a broken ankle, but, fortunately, life was restored to my extremities. I concluded my innings without further discomfort and shared a bottle of champagne with my delighted parents that evening. The following day I flew to London, had lunch at John Lawrence's home and met up with the Irish boys, Donal Lenihan and Ginger McLoughlan.

The three of us flew to New Zealand on the same plane as a supporters' party led by Gerald Davies. It could have developed into a very pleasant session on the flight but we three had to stay off the booze, which was quite a feat for Ginger.

On arrival, we had another flight from Auckland to Canterbury and, somewhat jet-lagged, met up with Willie John McBride, the tour manager, at 1 p.m. on a match day. He asked if I was prepared to sit on the bench and I said I didn't mind. He then reminded me that the match was against Canterbury, which meant I could find myself being called on in the first minute. Common sense told me there was nobody else to stand in if Roy Laidlaw got injured, so I was rushed to the ground, threw on Lions kit for the second time in my career and, also for the second time, went to sit on the replacements' bench for the Lions. Oddly enough, it happened to be the seat I had occupied ten years earlier when on tour with England.

164

As I settled on the bench I exchanged greetings with Ollie Campbell, who was sitting next to me, then with my old pal Dusty Hare and sat back, assuming Gwyn Evans was playing to take the kicks. I then turned round, saw Gwyn, and exchanged a greeting while trying to work out why, against a side as potentially dangerous as Canterbury, I was surrounded by world-class international goal kickers.

I asked Ollie who was taking the kicks and he told me Hugo McNeill was. When I said he had to be joking, Ollie told me Hugo had been hitting them rather well in training.

That's when I said, 'Ollie, I hate to tell my grandmother how to suck eggs but I am talking to one of the best kickers of all time and you know that hitting them in training is a bit different from the real thing.'

Poor Hugo missed three in the first quarter and the lads were well down after the game, which they lost. I felt particularly sorry for skipper Ciaran Fitzgerald. I had toured with him before and like the guy very much, but I felt that the one glaring omission from the Lions party was Peter Wheeler. The problem for Fitzie was that Britain had several world-class hookers and he would probably have been somewhere about fourth on that list.

But he had captained the side that had won the Five Nations championship the previous season and a trend seemed to have become established whereby the Lions job went to the player who had just led his country to success. I know it sounds ridiculous, but I could have been in the hot seat if England had beaten Wales that season and gone on to win the title. At the start of that season I had laughed at people who suggested I might end up as Lions captain because I firmly believe that job must go to a man who is capable of holding the Saturday spot without question. Can you imagine the pressure I would have been under, for instance, with a class player like Terry Holmes snapping at my heels? The situation would have been intolerable.

Any Lions captain should be a player who has already

had experience of a Lions tour and therefore gained an insight into what is involved. The selectors certainly had players available, like Peter Wheeler and Jeff Squire. Similarly, I believe Willie John, for whom I have the greatest respect, was, as tour manager, in the worst possible role for him. I would have preferred to have seen him as coach. I had no experience of Jim Telfer as a coach and didn't know what to expect. What I did know was that Scotland hadn't won too many pots at that stage.

I had decided right from the start of the tour that the only way to play the New Zealanders was with the action revolving around Terry Holmes and his back row, with Ollie left to slot the kicks. And the way the back row of Peter Winterbottom, Jeff Squire and John O'Driscoll started the tour, I thought we were at least in with a chance, especially with back-up of Jim Calder's calibre. If the front five could hold its own, we might just manage it.

With the first Test all those thoughts went right out of the window, especially as the Lions had travelled to New Zealand with, in my view, the wrong balance at scrum half. I'm not just saying that because I was involved, but it was essential to have a scrum half similar in style and physique to Terry Holmes. Someone like myself or one of a number who could play the game that way, such as David Bishop, from Pontypool, or Nick Youngs, from Leicester. As an alternative, they could have had Roy Laidlaw and Nigel Melville as a pair to play a very different type of game. The way things turned out, Roy wasn't physically strong enough to play the Holmes type of game and that played right into the hands of the All Blacks.

So, spirits were low after the Canterbury defeat and the usual singsong in the team room never materialized. Willie tried his best to lift the boys but they were quietly playing darts or drinking in small groups. Luckily, I spotted some mates from Bermuda and went out to join them for a drink. One or two of the lads came with us, we had a few laughs and it helped rescue the evening.

On the Saturday we were due to play the third Test at Dunedin and I had my first experience of a Jim Telfer coaching session. He had been nicknamed 'Creamy' and I soon discovered why. I considered it all effort and no direction: it was so frenetic that Jim finished up foaming at the mouth. From the comfort of my armchair back home I had watched Roy and Iain Paxton getting into a muddle at the base of the scrums and that would have been the first thing I would have sorted out. But nothing was done to improve that situation at the session, even though they had something like a hundred scrums in a hailstorm.

The lads lost the third Test at Dunedin in appalling conditions but their spirits were up because they had scored two tries. Yet, in truth, it was only the weather that saved them from a heavier defeat and when I had a chat with Andy Haden afterwards he said they knew it would be dry in Auckland for the final Test and were convinced they would give us a good hiding.

It was nice to see the lads looking a little happier because it's not much fun tramping around a country like that when you are being beaten. New Zealanders are not noted for showing you any mercy whatsoever. And not only were they hammering us 3–0 in the series at that stage, but they had also just beaten Australia in a cricket Test. Then I opened a newspaper one morning to discover that the Miss Universe title had been won by a New Zealander too. They were unbearable and I started to believe that God was a New Zealander.

When we arrived in Hawkes Bay for the next game we were called to the team room. When Willie John announced the side I very nearly fell off my perch. Not only was I to play my first game as a Lion, I was to do so as captain. Needless to say, I was profuse in my thanks to Willie John, but he told me that wasn't necessary. I had, he said, earned the honour and all he wanted was for me to 'go out and do it'.

The great thing about being made captain was that it

gave me a licence to speak and that is something I have always enjoyed doing at training sessions when I have felt there was a point that needed making. The first thing I did was to get the backs together because they hadn't been bringing the fullback into space properly. I wanted them to straighten the line by slowing down a little and they began to make headway. We started to get through an opposed midfield and Ollie admitted it was an improvement. It continued to go well until Jim marched over and started telling us to speed it up. When I told him we were trying to do exactly the opposite I got an earfull to the effect that I had only been there five minutes and was already trying to run the show.

Maybe I'm wrong, I don't know, but I have always believed that training sessions provide the opportunity to try different approaches and to encourage discussion between players and coach on ways to improve overall team performance. For all the training sessions we had we never really got down to talking about the things we should have been correcting until the day of the game. It was all 100 m.p.h. stuff with no real detail.

When match day dawned it was red hot, the pitch was like concrete and, although fit, I hadn't trained to quite the same high standard during the three weeks when it looked as though I wasn't going to be needed by the Lions, at any price. Needless to say, I found the game very hard, but as it unfolded it turned into a cracking contest with Hawkes Bay playing above themselves and the Lions playing somewhat below par. Still, we won, giving me a 100 per cent record as a Lions captain!

I thought I would get a break for the next game but I was selected for the Saturday side and that led to a good deal of speculation that I might be chosen in the Test side the following week – which would have been a real turn-up for the book. That story was helped along by Roy's condition. He looked well beaten and because of the injuries to Terry and Nigel the poor lad had played something like thirteen games. He hadn't the physical presence to take all that and he was going through a really rough patch. The battering can't have helped him much psychologically either. Meanwhile, I came through my second game well enough and speculation increased, even though I was so stiff I could hardly walk.

We travelled to Hamilton the next day and just when I should have been resting tired muscles, Jim had us straight out doing sprints. I was paired with Jim Calder and as I could ill afford to be seen to be ten yards slower than a back-row forward, I had to pull out the stops. In the first sprint I could feel one of my hamstrings and had an immediate chat with Kevin Murphy, the Lions physiotherapist, who is a Sale clubmate of mine and knows my hamstrings as well as anybody. He shook his head, because he wasn't happy, but I went ahead with the second sprint and had to pull up. Frustratingly, I have been plagued by that hamstring ever since.

As I limped off for treatment the lads all shouted, 'Skiver,' but I knew that my chances of playing in the Test had become remote. I needed a lot of treatment to have a chance of playing, but Roy settled the issue by turning in a fine performance four days before the Test. It may sound an awful thing to say, but that was the only time in my life I have sat in a dressing room and not been desperate to get into the side.

I wasn't terribly happy at the thought of my hamstring having to survive a full eighty minutes and in terms of the game's outcome I'm afraid the writing was on the wall for the lads. Preparations were as frenetic as ever and, as usually happens when things are going wrong, the lads started breaking up into little discussion groups, each coming up with its own theories as to what had gone wrong, and why. I think if they had had to place their hands on hearts, every single one of them knew they had no chance in the final Test.

By that stage in the tour the Lions were inferior to the All Blacks; it was a very different situation from South Africa in 1980 when the Lions prevented a whitewash by winning the last Test. On that occasion the lads knew they had literally thrown away the first three Tests, but in New Zealand the Lions had been outplayed. The All Blacks knew it and they couldn't wait to get the opposition on firm ground. They knew they hadn't played well in the first Test, which the Lions could have won; the wind during the second Test was so strong even the posts wouldn't stay still; and in Dunedin they needed underwater oilskins to keep warm.

When Test day dawned in Auckland the sun was cracking the flags. And blow me, if I wasn't in the same seat I had sat in to watch England's victory over New Zealand in 1973. I could almost picture Fran Cotton running down the touchline, selling outrageous dummies and putting in a beautiful cross kick in the dying seconds of the game.

At the kick-off, Gary Whetton took the ball on the rattle, ploughed through our pack, trampling all over little Roy in the process and leaving him writhing on the ground in agony. The All Blacks won five rucks in rapid succession and should have scored three tries, but somehow we kept them out. All I could do was stare at Roy, who hadn't moved. I thought, Oh my God. He's not getting up.

The referee had blown for a scrum, Roy was still on the deck and I started slapping Deep Heat on my hamstring. Nick Jeavons told me what a lucky bastard I was because it looked as though I was certain to be taking the field and I told him the best place for us that afternoon might well be the seats we were sitting in. As I stripped off my tracksuit and the lads on the bench wished me luck, I determined I was going to go out there and give it the very best shots I had ever given anything. Then, bugger me, Roy pops up and trots off to the scrum. I settled back to watch the inevitable humiliation.

New Zealand scored a couple of tries, were very quickly out of sight, and you don't need me to take you through the agonies of what happened thereafter. The Lions were heading for their heaviest Test defeat. The game was finished as a spectacle very quickly and the later stages were played in almost total silence, with ripples of polite applause when New Zealand scored. It was like watching a funeral.

The situation afterwards was desperate. After all, what on earth can you say to comfort one another? You are all together, a long way from home and nobody wants to know you. Poor old Fritzie. I think the lad was destroyed and what annoys me is the way he got all the flak rather than the faceless people who had put him into an untenable situation. People in New Zealand thought we were the pits, to coin John McEnroe's phrase, but I think the right side, with the right captain and management, would have fared rather better. I'm not saying the Lions would have won the series, but it would have been a close-run thing.

The itinerary the Four Home Unions had agreed to was a very tough one and in those circumstances personnel became very important. It said something for the state of affairs that the physio, Kevin Murphy, was voted personality of the tour by three of the press gang. Kev was good value, he worked hard, he certainly played hard and he kept the lads going. I wouldn't like to think where they would have been without him. There was hardly anyone else who could raise our spirits. That's why it was always good to have a player like Mickey Burton in the party because nothing ever seemed to get him down and he would make light of adversity.

There were no Sunday Schools on tour. These are totally spontaneous Sunday drinking sessions that have become something of a tradition on long tours but tend to be a feature that evolves because the players want it. On that tour it didn't happen, which possibly says something for the mood of the party and the lack of characters. I know this may sound stupid and leave people thinking of rugby players as terribly immature, but there comes a time when you need to let off steam. I don't think players should be expected to train on Sundays while touring, especially on a tour as hard as that one. The lads take a physical hammering – everybody wants to beat the Lions – and they need the

171

occasional break to relax and unwind.

Willie John was good value in the sense that he took some of the touring pressure off the players. He tried to keep them away from evening functions, normally dinners and receptions, and did most of that ambassadorial work himself. He was a real trojan in that respect and I'm not sure if the lads realized just how much weight he took off their shoulders. The one thing he insisted on the players doing was the round of school trips, which are made during the morning. I wonder how some of the players, unaccustomed to public speaking, coped with giving a talk to an assembly hall filled with seven hundred schoolchildren.

After that desperate final Test I sat and chatted with Murray Mexted, who asked where we were stopping off en route to England. He assumed we would have a few days to unwind in either Fiji or Los Angeles and couldn't believe we weren't going somewhere to soak up the sun and sprawl on a beach. A tour of that severity, and in a New Zealand winter, really warranted that sort of bonus for the players.

On the flight home I sat with Jim Telfer. It was the first time we had got together for a serious chat and I wondered what lessons would be learned. I suspected that his report, along with that of Willie John, would probably be handed to the committee, whoever they were, and left to gather dust.

Planning and preparation could be so much better throughout this game of ours, but I had no complaints about the build-up to my next meeting with the All Blacks. That was when the North played the tourists at Gateshead early in the 1983–84 season; it promised to be an interesting confrontation bearing in mind what the North had done to their pride at Otley four years previously. They were without several important players, but we had probably lost even more talent than they had and we couldn't have been expected to repeat the success of Otley. Even so, there was no way the region was going to let the All Blacks walk all over its chosen fifteen.

The planning for that game was brilliant. As captain I was included in selection discussions and although I don't think a captain deserves a vote in a side like that I do think his opinion should be sought and listened to. On that occasion I was asked about Paul Simpson, the Bath number 8, who went on to play flanker for England. Although I hadn't seen him play that season I knew he was a bloody good player and was able to say so. My observations may, or may not, have influenced his selection, but I'm sure I tipped the scales with centre Tony Bond. He wasn't even in the Lancashire side at the time but was playing well for Sale and was the type of hard, committed player you need to face the All Blacks.

The important thing is that we talked. The North was also fortunate in having Mike Weston as chairman of selectors, Dave Robinson as coach, and selectors as experienced in the modern game as Tony Neary and Peter Dixon. We talked about the team and we talked about the itinerary. We talked at length about the opposition and about the tactics that might best be employed against them.

Everything went like clockwork, the lads played above themselves, we had the All Blacks on the rack for half an hour and in the end lost quite narrowly. London should have beaten them and it was always on the cards that the Midlands would. They had the team to do it, and they did, laying the foundations for England's subsequent victory.

I knew I was in with a good chance of an England recall until the Midlands game in which Nick Youngs played the right tactics and made pretty sure of his place in the national side. My hopes really lay with my old adversary and partner, Johnny Horton. Had he played very well for the South West against the tourists we may very well have returned to the England side as a pairing. Unfortunately for me, he didn't have one of his better games and I ended up on the England replacements' bench. I had no arguments about that because the

173

selectors had followed advice they had to some extent
ignored four years previously by picking players who had
recently posed problems for the tourists and exposed
some of their weaknesses.

I would have loved another outing in an England shirt
but, knowing my seesaw luck, I haven't yet given up
hope of one last fling!

12

Ten Number Nines

One of the reasons rugby is such a marvellous game is that it has something to offer for widely differing skills, physiques and temperaments. An 18-stone prop has a role to play that is just as important as that played by a ballerina of a fly half; in the same way, courage and strength of will might make one a great player while the motivating force of fear might be a useful part of an elusive back's make-up.

Scrum half, for instance, was the ideal position for me, suiting my physique, ability level and temperament. Many top-class halfbacks also display a talent on the soccer field where many of them develop balance, timing and vision long before they ever get their hands on a rugby ball. With the spread of mini rugby that situation will change, but soccer was the game played by the masses when I was a youngster. As for temperament, anyone who knows me even remotely well will tell you that I am a fairly chirpy chap with a highly competitive edge and you will find most decent scrum halves coming from that particular mould.

One thing he must have is the basic skill of passing. The ability to kick is equally crucial and without those skills a scrum half isn't going to progress very far. If he also happens to be either strong enough or sharp enough to produce a defence-splitting break as well, then that is a bonus because he automatically increases his side's scoring opportunities. Over the years I have come across hundreds of players with those skills but at that stage another dimension creeps in – the ability to make the right decision at the right time. The truly great scrum halves have all had that same hallmark of knowing exactly how and when to use those skills.

I have always found it interesting to look back at some of the world-class scrum halves I have tangled with, trying to compile a list in order of merit based on my own observations. Not an easy task because all had, or still have, different strengths but few weaknesses.

After much deliberation I arrived at my personal top ten, which should provide the basis for discussion!

1 Gareth Edwards (Wales)
2 Dave Loveridge (New Zealand)
3 Sid Going (New Zealand)
4 Mark Donaldson (New Zealand)
5 Terry Holmes (Wales)
6 Max Barrau (France)
7 Colin Patterson (Ireland)
8 Jérôme Gallion (France)
9 Jan Webster (England)
10 John Hipwell (Australia)

A formidable list and a great array of talent, but the player who stood out from all the others was Gareth. He was, without question, the best rugby player I have ever seen – and that includes both codes of rugby. What amazed me about him was his strength. I have always considered myself a fairly strong player and it has always suited me to play against scrum halves who are strong, but he was exceptional. And that point was illustrated for me when we swopped shirts on one occasion; when I put his on it literally drowns me, with the shoulders finishing about halfway down my biceps.

Gareth was a real barrel of a man and yet his pace was truly incredible. He was a good 200-metre sprinter and on Lions tours he was known to outsprint wingers in training. I decided a long time ago that he just had to be a freak of nature.

A truly great player in my book is one without a weakness and Gareth Edwards falls clearly into that category. You only had to be in the England dressing room during the late sixties and early seventies to realize what an immense presence he had in the game. The England players were quite paranoid about him and their sole topic of conversation used to be how to stop him.

There was more to Gareth than his devastating break and that's why he was a lethal opponent. The uninitiated might be surprised to learn that it is not terribly difficult to prevent a scrum half breaking from the base of a scrum. All you need is the ploy John Scott and I used effectively against class players and strong breakers such as Terry Holmes. We would simply ask for the scrum to be wheeled to close down the channel through which a scrum half can break.

With Gareth, however, you might finish a game and be able to claim he had never made one break against you, only to have to concede that he had probably won the game with his kicking instead. He was also one of the few players you could never completely clamp down; he always seemed to be able to produce the crucial break when necessary. There was also the important factor of his diverting attention from other quality players outside him, who would enjoy a greater degree of freedom because the opposition would be focusing their energies on the man in the number 9 shirt.

There are some people who claim that Terry Holmes is a better player. All I can say is that they have short memories. I'm not knocking Terry for one minute and the two of us have talked about it so I'm not saying anything new for his ears. Terry is a tremendous player, as strong as Gareth and probably as elusive. But he doesn't quite have Gareth's all-round skill.

I have heard others criticize Gareth's passing, saying he didn't pass the ball quickly. Perhaps he didn't pass the ball quickly but you have to remember that during the period when he was playing the long spin pass was in fashion. In the eyes of selectors, coaches, players and the public, the farther you threw the ball the better. We all adopted that style at the time. But if Gareth pulled on a pair of shorts tomorrow and took the field he would very quickly be passing with Dave Loveridge dexterity. He would simply have adopted to whatever style of pass was in vogue and it is worthy of mention that he started out with an indifferent service but worked at it until it was perfect.

One of the first occasions I studied Gareth was while I was at Loughborough and I watched an international against Scotland when Lewis Dick, who was also at Loughborough, came on as a replacement. The one thing we were sure of was that Lewis could shift because Jim Greenwood used to have us sprinting between lamp posts up a local hill every day. We were all fairly sharp then but Lewis, with the exception of Clive Rees, was the quickest mover in the squad.

As we watched on television, Gareth suddenly chipped over Lewis and gave chase. Lewis turned to go after him and I sat with my mouth open as Gareth took yards off him. It was then I realized just how much pace he had and that, coupled with his powerful, stocky frame, made him a pretty formidable spectacle.

Like all great players he underwent a subtle change as he grew older. Just like those two marvellous Rugby League halfbacks, Alex Murphy and Roger Millward, as his pace reduced so his tactical awareness became even better.

The thing I always envied him was his ability to kick with pinpoint accuracy with his right foot. If I could have had a wish granted it would be to have possessed the two natural assets vital to a scrum half – to be left-handed and right-footed. From a scrum you are invariably passing with your left hand and using your right foot to kick for touch or into the box. Most of my left-footed kicking has been from lineout, ruck and maul or from a scrum when the number 8 has flicked it up to me standing back. Gareth had that important right foot.

He was also incredibly durable, which he needed to be to win fifty-three Welsh caps. One or two people sniped at him and suggested he looked after himself by limiting the number of games he played for Cardiff, but they are inclined to forget that rugby is a terribly hard game and he was the number one target in the world. In every game in which he played he was a marked man. He was under continual pressure and I believe the fact he escaped injuries had something to do with his marvellous vision. People with good peripheral vision, as he clearly had, tend not to get injured too often. They become aware of what is about to happen a split second ahead of the average player.

When I damaged my hamstring playing for Lancashire against Surrey in the county championship first division play-off at Blundellsands towards the end of 1983, I was hit from behind by Francis Emeruwa, of Wasps. I didn't even know he was there and the tackle was totally unexpected. Players with good vision normally see a tackle coming and ride it.

So I don't go along with criticism of Gareth on any score. He is a great bloke, a typically chirpy scrum half, and there wasn't a chink in his playing armour.

Looking for a runner-up led me into a direct choice between two All Blacks; it is significant that three New Zealanders take three of the top four places. The choice for second spot was between Sid Going and Dave Loveridge and at first I thought the former had the edge purely on the grounds that he was so difficult to play against. But on balance I decided Gareth's runner-up had to be Dave, who is more adaptable and a beautiful footballer.

Dave is a very different kettle of fish to Sid. He has the ability to adapt to any kind of game and although he can't drive at people the way Sid used to do, he uses his pace to go wide from the set piece so that he had the option of flicking the ball out or back inside again. As the 1983 Lions discovered to their cost, he has a great pair of hands and keeps the ball alive. His other great strength is as a tactician and in that department I would place him even ahead of Gareth. There isn't much in it, but he is marginally better tactically.

His service is also just right. It's not too short or too long and it travels very quickly through the air. If I had my time all over again, Dave is the player I would copy. He is as quick as lightning off both hands, extremely accurate, and moves the ball off the deck like a bullet. Mind you, it helps when you know where the ball is going to be and that's never a problem for a New Zealand scrum half.

In Britain you sometimes get the ball in the air and sometimes on the ground. And how you receive it makes a hell of a difference as you approach a maul. If a player is going to feed it to you, it's necessary to stand off a good yard, but if the ball is on the ground you have to go in and pluck it out. When I arrived in New Zealand as a replacement on the 1983 Lions tour I was taking part in my first training session and Peter Winterbottom and a couple of the other players turned in a maul to face me. I automatically took a step back to receive the pass. As I did so they threw the ball on the floor and I asked them what they were doing. They said, 'Rucking.' New Zealand scrum halves have the advantage of knowing exactly where the ball is going every time and I am convinced we will have to adapt to the rucking game eventually.

I thought Loveridge was the man of the 1983 Test series. He was tactically dominant and when the All Blacks came over here later that year without their normal front five and Loveridge, he was the player they missed most.

In my book it was a tight contest between Dave and Sid Going and, although I wouldn't describe Going, a stroppy little Maori, as a complete scrum half, he was razor sharp and probably the best breaker on my list. He suited New Zealand's style of play perfectly because he was low to the ground and was a tremendous rucker.

It was fascinating to watch him because whenever he broke and was stopped you could lay money on Ian Kirkpatrick being right up behind him to take the ball and continue the move, with Going then going off in support of his flanker. People like to talk about great halfback partnerships, but Sid's was different. His partner was Kirkpatrick!

Going was a better kicker than people gave him credit for being and he was a very astute tactician. Although his service wasn't great, it wasn't bad either, but if we look for a weakness it must be that he could be blocked out. It was a very difficult thing to do but when it happened it invariably put the opposition in the driving seat.

I remember the British Lions pack playing superbly in the second Test during the 1977 series and I received a letter from Fran saying that Going had been dropped. He thought the selectors had made a major mistake and was convinced that would help the Lions wrap up the series. But, as Fran and the rest of us discovered to our cost, the selectors hadn't blundered at all. On the contrary, they had been extremely astute. They realized that if they couldn't come up with a pack to beat the Lions they would have to unload one of the biggest names in the game and bring in Canterbury scrum half, Lyn Davis, to play a more expansive type of game. Lyn's quick service enabled the New Zealanders to switch the emphasis of their game and they won the series. It was a marvellous piece of selection and I couldn't help thinking that had the same thing happened in Britain we would have reacted in the opposite way and started dropping props.

Not far behind either Loveridge or Going I would place Mark Donaldson. He had the edge over Loveridge for a spell and he is younger. I played against him when the North beat the All Blacks at Otley and rated Dave and him as the two best scrum halves in the world at that time.

Donaldson was another magnificent passer of a ball and although his reaction time was fractionally slower than Loveridge's, it still travelled through the air like a rocket. Even though the wind was making passing very difficult that day he was still flinging the ball out with uncanny accuracy. He was a very aggressive player and more of a handful than Dave, but lacked his tactical awareness.

No doubt some of you will be surprised that I have placed those three All Blacks ahead of Terry Holmes but I believe New Zealand is the country that produces the best scrum halves these days. Terry was under a lot of pressure on the 1983 Lions tour, until his injury, and he is always going to have a problem in New Zealand because of his build. He is a physical player but New Zealanders are well equipped to cope with that and they might have been more vulnerable confronted by a Dave Loveridge type of player.

Compared to Gareth his shape is all wrong. He has long legs and that makes it easier to stop him. Whenever we played against each other I would always go for his ankles; it wasn't as easy to stop Gareth that way because he was such a short-arse he would never leave footprints in the desert. Where players make a mistake with Terry is in trying to tackle him high. If you do that you have no chance because he is terribly strong and very, very committed.

Having told you how to stop him (at close range) you might be wondering why I place him as high as fifth, but that is simply because he is a match winner. He reminds me of a soccer striker in that, no matter what else happens, he's going to score. That is something he invariably does from close in and people ought to study his tries to see how cleverly he does it. I always used to tell the England players not to make the mistake of thinking that, because of his size and strength, he will go for the head-on clash when he tries to reach the line. Terry is too clever for that and instead he picks the ball out, looks for his spot and then, as cool as a cucumber, actually takes his time. Rather than rush headlong for the line he gives a little jink to throw you off balance, and then he has got you. It's like watching a spider coax a fly into its web.

Terry has a lovely sidestep and it has caught out some of the best in the business. During the 1977 meeting between England and Wales he left Mike Rafter for dead at a set piece and I use that incident to illustrate the point because Mike is one of the best tackling wing forwards I have ever played against. He wasn't an easy player to outmanoeuvre and on the occasions I played against him I never tried to make a break down his side of the scrum.

Getting down to basics, Terry is a better kicker than people realize and the right-foot chip which he chases himself is very effective. Of the top five he is probably the worst passer but compensates by being a real handful out on the park. He is a big-hearted lad, both on and off the field, and I really like the guy. When we were in Cape Town together a couple of years ago he kept taking on the opposition and getting knocked over for his pains and I asked him why he didn't change his tactics. Honest lad that he is, he told me he had considered alternatives but tended to lose a fraction of a second reaching a decision on the options open to him. He was, he said, an instinctive player and accepted the situation.

French scrum halves put the fear of God into me because they are always razor sharp. Because it is one of my weaknesses I have always worried about opponents who are very quick off the mark and, against the French, I bank on a good pack to provide a solid platform. Then I am able to dominate the scrum half physically because they tend not to have an awful lot of bottle compared to some of the tough little nuts I have come up against over the years.

The French scrum half I respect most is Max Barrau, who once practically beat the All Blacks single-handed. I played against him at Twickenham in only my second international and Peter Dixon and I were given the task of marking him out of the game. As things turned out he went off injured but before that he made one break up the touchline that left Peter and myself for dead. The speed of the man was incredible and there was relief all round when the cover cut him off before he could escape completely.

The luckless Colin Patterson has to figure in my top ten. Stocky and a good all-rounder with a lovely service and an electrically quick break, Colin had a size that belied his strength. He was definitely not the sort of player you could brush off. A real Irish terrier, in fact.

I felt terribly sorry for him when he damaged knee ligaments so badly during the 1980 Lions tour of South Africa that his career was over. The injury meant that I was called out to sit on the replacements' bench for the final Test but I would much rather have stayed at home and seen a fit Colin taking on the Springboks.

He had a magnificent try-scoring record for Ireland and was averaging one a game when he first got into the Irish side. A really genuine lad off the field, I thoroughly enjoyed his company and we sat together in the Hilton one night after we had played against each other at Twickenham and quietly demolished a bottle of port as we set the world to rights.

The second Frenchman to get into my top ten is Jérôme Gallion, who re-emerged again last season after a three-year absence. Had he stayed around he would have been a truly great player by now, but when I faced him during our Grand Slam run he was having a bit of a downer and the French press were getting at him.

As we were dominating things up front that afternoon the poor lad got rather swamped and, in typical French style, spent most of his time berating his pack. He was only a youngster then and, with his tremendous pace, seemed a great prospect for the future. He also has a nice service off both hands, which makes him something of an exception to the rule because French scrum halves tend to be rather poor passers of the ball.

Only one English scrum half of my era gets into the frame. It shouldn't take a clairvoyant to help you guess that I am going unhesitatingly for my old adversary, Jan Webster. I may not have placed him at number one, but in one area he most definitely was because I have never seen a better scrum half behind a beaten pack.

Little Jan was built for the job and he had courage

grafted on in large helpings. He was an immaculate kicker – the Springboks and All Blacks will vouch for that – and had the ability to dominate a game. Irony takes a hand too as he had a very quick service but played at a time when the long pass was regarded as the ultimate weapon in a scrum half's artillery. If he were still playing at the highest level today people would be raving about the quality of his service, but, with the selectorial battering he took, he is probably philosophical enough to be able to say, 'That's life.'

It is unfortunate that his two great performances were both overseas and unseen by the folks back home. I was on the bench for the victories over South Africa in 1972 and New Zealand a year later and I can tell you that Jan's performances were as good as any produced either before, or since, by an England scrum half. On each occasion the opposition had a fullback making his debut and our forwards were playing out of their skulls. That was a situation Jan simply revelled in. He possessed a beautiful box kick and spent the afternoon pumping the ball into the air and the opposition spent the afternoon dropping it. And when you think about it, that was a very effective way of playing your rugby.

Yet, like myself, Jan had a very in and out international career. It was criminal the way England selectors wasted their material.

The last name on my list might cause a few raised eyebrows amongst those who would have placed him rather higher. Well, I played against John Hipwell three times and, while there was no doubting his class, he had the same fault that afflicts most Australian scrum halves – his pass was too short. People talk about the marvellous flick pass favoured by the Aussies, but I'm not in the least impressed. It's the pass favoured by many Rugby League scrum halves and I could teach someone to do it in no time at all. It might work all right in Rugby League but in that game the fly half doesn't have a great big open-side wing forward breathing down his neck all afternoon.

185

The ability to move the ball quickly is a valuable asset but the Aussies tend to do it slavishly without getting anywhere in particular. Unless a player is prepared to commit an opponent, all that happens is that everyone ends up tumbling into touch. I played against them three times one season and they never once made a break from a tight situation.

Where Hipwell impressed me was in his tactical play. He was often playing behind a beaten Aussie pack but still came out well on the credit side. His other quality was durability; he was around the international scene for a very long time, and was able to fall back on his tactical skills once the edge had gone off his pace.

The players I have discussed all had the basics right and that is the first requirement of a scrum half. Unfortunately, many of the home-grown scrum halves I have come up against in recent seasons just haven't had the basics and that's why Nigel Melville stuck out like a sore thumb. He clearly had the ability to succeed at the highest level because his basics were so good and that is the ability people recognize when they see him play.

He can have a poor game but you can guarantee he will still pass the ball out beautifully. Dave Loveridge set the pattern for today's young players and, as a passer of the ball, I don't think Nigel is far behind him. The big question mark so far as Nigel is concerned is going to be in relation to his strength. He is only slightly built and, with the attention he will always receive from other scrum halves and back-row forwards, injuries may be a problem.

Scrum halves tend to be bigger these days and even small lads like Jan Webster and Colin Patterson were pretty stocky, with powerful shoulders. Nick Youngs, of Leicester, who eventually replaced me in the England side when Nigel was injured, has the strength to compete at that level although, in fairness, I have never seen Nick as England's long-term answer.

Which reminds me of an amusing moment in the Sale clubhouse on the day of this year's England trial when I was still out of action with a hamstring injury. A match report was being broadcast and the commentator was saying that Nick hadn't had a terribly good game and that the selectors must be hoping that – at that point everybody turned to look at me – Nigel Melville was fit!

Everyone burst out laughing, but I felt for Nick. After all, he had just played the game of his life against the All Blacks (twice) and was being written off straightaway. If it's any consolation to the lad, we have all suffered at the hands of those who think they know best.

13

Now, Let There Be Light

Harold Macmillan once talked about the wind of change blowing through Africa, Donovan once strained his vocal chords telling us 'the times they are a changing' and, whether we like it or not, the wind of change has started to ruffle a few Rugby Union feathers. Those of us who genuinely love the game can only pray that change comes about without the roof being blown off.

There are, of course, those who would like to see the lid removed from what they regard as a can of worms in the hope that our great amateur game will be laid bare to reveal a monetary honey pot into which just about everybody is dipping his sticky fingers. There are those outside the game who would like nothing better than to find a chink in our amateur armour and there are others, within the game, who are so paranoid about possible tarnish by filthy lucre that they have about the same appeal as a totally bigoted Afrikaner.

As usual, things tend to be treated out of all proportion and although there is a very definite change taking place in Rugby Union it is not of the enormity some people would care to believe and is eminently controllable if everybody uses common sense.

Change has started to come about because of the people who play the modern game. Time was when Rugby Union, by and large, was the preserve of those who had attended public or grammar schools. That, in itself, helped to create a fairly definite social barrier but, with the change to comprehensive education and the strengthening of colts and junior rugby, the game has evolved in such a way that social barriers no longer exist. The whole spectrum of rugby has now opened up and the reason there are problems today is that those running the game are generally of the old public and grammar school stock.

That is not meant as a criticism, merely a statement of fact. I am not one of those who goes along with the view that those running our game are a bunch of throwbacks and idiots, even though I have had my brushes with some of them over the years. There are many intelligent men in the RFU who genuinely care for the game. I have always placed RFU secretary, Bob Weighill, in that category. He is a man I have always been able to get along with and that may have something to do with the fact that I found him extremely open for someone in his position and with his background. Nor is he anybody's fool, but he is, at least, very sensible, gentlemanly, polite and a thoroughly nice person to deal with. I have often chatted to him about problems and we have talked freely together about the David Lord affair since the moment it raised its head.

Others on the committee can be categorized along with Bob but, if they were all asked their views on how they thought the game should develop, it would almost certainly differ from the views of the modern player. And, at present, they are controlling the game and it will only develop in the way they want it to. The immediate future is very much in their hands and I don't think we will see too much by way of change while they are in control.

Some changes will have to come about, however, and it is obviously preferable for everyone concerned if those changes come from the top rather than from outside the game altogether. The changes don't have to be quite as dramatic as the deeply entrenched brigade probably imagine. They would merely be changes necessary for bringing the game fully into the twentieth century. And by that I don't mean lining the players' pockets.

If clubs had to pay their players the game would be

dead within months, but, unless the amateur laws are relaxed a little, we will continue to lose players of the highest possible calibre who would have otherwise been available to serve the game in any number of ways after they had retired from the playing arena.

I find it terribly sad, nay, ridiculous, that players like Bill Beaumont and Fran Cotton, to name but two, should be lost to the game because they capitalized, to some extent, on their names after injury had forced both reluctantly to hang up their boots. Yet neither had benefited materially while playing Rugby Union. It's little wonder players, seeing the treatment meted out to that illustrious and highly respected pair, should think seriously about saying to hell with it and taking up an offer that would be likely to make their futures financially secure.

I do not hide the fact that I was one of the players contacted by David Lord when he came to Britain to promote his revolutionary plan for a professional Rugby Union circus. We had met in Australia three years earlier so it was fairly natural that I should figure on his list of people to look up.

It is a strange experience to receive a telephone call from someone who asks what you are planning to do during the following twelve months. When you tell him you don't really know and he then suggests he would like to fly you around the world for two years playing international standard rugby and putting £100,000 in your pocket at the same time, you tend to drop the telephone ... and then pick it up again as quickly as reflexes allow.

That is exactly how he launched his ambitious scheme into my ordered little world and we eventually came face to face in a Cheshire hotel. With me were other England players who had been approached and we listened to what he had to say. We also fired a few questions at him and later discussed the scheme amongst ourselves and attempted to put the whole thing into perspective. By doing so we all, to the best of my knowledge, came to the same conclusion. That was that if David Lord ever came up with a firm contract we would each have a very important decision to make.

Until such a stage was reached the whole thing was totally hypothetical; in terms of jeopardizing our amateur status it was no different from being approached by a Rugby League scout. If you live and play in the north you soon become used to receiving visits and telephone calls from gentlemen within the professional game. They sound out players to see if there is a flicker of interest in playing Rugby League and follow our game so closely they know exactly when a top Union player is most vulnerable – normally when he is out of favour with selectors!

There were people who, having heard David Lord's scheme, imagined players would leave Rugby Union in droves in order to pocket very substantial amounts of cash. Fortunately there were others who did not over-dramatize the situation and Bob Weighill was one of those. He knew full well that David's scheme wasn't as simple as it sounded.

Perhaps we should consider my own case. I had just started a new job with Bukta, who manufacture sports gear. The company had been through a rough patch but there was a new management team, business was picking up and expanding and, quite apart from enjoying the work immensely, I was being offered a good, sound career in an area of business that interested me most, for obvious reasons. As my playing career had already entered its 'twilight years' and the future was starting to become more important to me, I would have had an extremely difficult decision to make. But, rest assured, I wasn't prepared to rush into something that might never take off and which, at the very least, would have been a risky venture. I know I speak for other players when I say that an enormous amount of money would have to have been put up front before any of us got down to thinking that seriously about it.

Bob Weighill got in touch with me when the Lord plan

hit the newspapers and asked if I had been approached. I saw no point in lying about it and told him that David had been in contact with me; I was, after all, a fairly obvious person to be in touch with bearing in mind that my career as a senior player didn't have all that long to run. We discussed the whole thing sensibly and both realized that for the scheme to get off the ground David would need to raise in the region of £30 million. An enormous sum by any standards.

The initial reaction of players was that they would probably be unable to turn down the offer if the money really was as good as suggested and was guaranteed. If there are people who deplore that attitude, then all I can say is that they must be in an extremely fortunate position for £100,000 not to mean a great deal to them. But so far as present-day players are concerned, it is an absolute fortune. No player I know can think in terms of earning six figures within just two years.

Despite the paranoia in some circles, the David Lord circus would not have posed a threat to Rugby Union unless rule changes made professional rugby more of a spectacle and people suddenly stopped attending international matches at Twickenham. The truth is that the RFU and the International Board have a product they don't have to improve and don't have to market. Twickenham is filled to capacity at least twice a year. Money pours into the coffers by way of ticket applications, and three months – and a good deal of interest – later, tickets are sent out and vast amounts of surplus cash refunded. Perhaps the RFU should write a book called *How To Succeed Without Trying*.

If all the top players suddenly rushed off to play professional rugby the effect on the game would be minimal. If I was one of those who took off, Sale would still train during the summer and play Morley in the opening match of every season. Merely launching a professional rugby circus wouldn't seriously affect Rugby Union as we know it. If the best players in the world were playing in a professional tournament at Old Deer

Park, Richmond, on the afternoon of an England *v.* Wales match at Twickenham, I bet that Twickenham would be packed to capacity as usual. The only way a venture such as David Lord proposed could pose a threat would be if the laws were changed to some degree, the circus was marketed properly and presented very well on television.

So far as the laws are concerned, Rugby Union is a very complex game and people don't often know exactly what is going on, including the players. The game has become whistle happy to a ridiculous extent. If a professional promoter were able to simplify the game without losing certain key elements, which are missing from Rugby League to that game's detriment, he might just pose the sort of threat I suggested earlier.

Professional Rugby Union would have to grab the interest of the paying public. That will always be a possibility while viewing figures for the amateur game on television are terrible, with the exception of those few Saturdays in a season when international matches are televised live. In those games standards don't seem as important, especially for those who attend them. They are very much social occasions and form has little to do with attendance. The 1983 Ireland *v.* England match in Dublin was one of the worst games I have ever seen at that level yet the attitude of the spectators was, 'Pity about the game, see you in two years.'

With astute law changes and proper marketing techniques, Rugby Union still has the potential to be the greatest spectator sport. That is probably what attracted David Lord and will doubtless attract other entrepreneurs in the future.

There is a good deal of interest in professional rugby in New Zealand and Australia where the approach to the amateur game is rather different from ours, but I don't think there would be a major upheaval Down Under if professional Rugby Union got off the ground. There, as in France, they are fairly professional anyway. And that must be a matter of some concern at Twickenham.

The difficulty comes in trying to define exactly where amateurism ends and professionalism begins. Top rugby players these days tend to get quite well looked after and are offered jobs they would probably not have been offered but for the fact that they were international rugby players.

Success tends to breed further success, placing a young player in the public limelight, and he finds himself on a roundabout that is extremely difficult to get off. When you first start playing rugby at the age of eleven you don't expect to end up playing for England and being subjected to pressures you haven't been groomed for. The average international rugby player is just an ordinary chap, following a normal career and possibly trying to raise a young family – unlike a professional sportsman who knows full well the moment he signs his contract that he has become a commercial commodity.

The modern game and its leading participants receive exposure that wasn't evident twenty or thirty years ago when most of today's administrators were involved as players. And whether those authorities like it or not, their present-day counterparts are the recipients of unsolicited gifts. The minute a young player arrives at the top, people want to give him boots, bags, airline tickets to distant places and cash.

After I had led England to victory over Wales at Twickenham in 1982 I was late leaving the ground because of the press conference and other matters in which an international captain gets involved. I was carrying bags in both hands and had to run through the crowds to the team coach. As I did so people were shoving ten-pound notes into my pockets as though it were a Greek wedding. They were delighted at our victory, were telling me how well we had done and to buy the lads a few beers. By the time I reached the team coach money was spilling from my pockets. That happened as part of the general euphoria of the occasion, but, looked at in the strictest possible way, it was a mild form of professionalism. In that crowd it was impossible

194

identifying the hands thrusting money into your pocket so there was only one thing to do: make sure the lads enjoyed free booze later as the spoils of battle.

Generally speaking, players don't go looking for rewards from the game. The rewards go looking for them and it is impossible to avoid them, especially if you are playing in countries like Wales, France, New Zealand and Australia. The number of players affected is very, very small in relation to the game as a whole, but those players are put under pressure by the existing laws and it is difficult to know how to handle the situation.

One or two players go over the top and become greedy, but they are the exception to the rule; most of the lads I know give an enormous amount back to the game in terms of time. The demands on a top player's time these days would scare off a professional and when we talk to professional sportsmen at functions they clearly think we are off our rockers. The hours devoted to training and squad sessions are frightening when you consider that rugby players have jobs just like the man in the street. More time is spent in travelling and those who fire arrows should try driving from Gosforth to Stourbridge and back again for an evening squad session. Players continually turn out in charity games on Sundays, the one day in the week when they might have the opportunity to spend some time with their families, and invitations to speak at dinners are never ending.

Oddly, only players seem to be open to criticism. The first hint of any compensation for time and effort and the individual concerned is branded as greedy and a disgrace to the game. Yet those same people would expect a player to drive 200 miles in his precious free time, to speak at a dinner attended by people he had never seen before in his life, spend the night at the home of a total stranger or in a hotel and then drive the 200 miles back home. There are many kind and considerate people in this game of ours, don't get me wrong, but there are others who seem to think they own shares in you once you rise to international standard.

There are those whose sole interest in life seems to be to catch a player with his hands in the honey pot and, unfortunately, a few intent on stabbing a player in the back without any justification whatsoever. After the 1983 Lions tour I had to travel down to the East India Club to appear before the RFU amateur laws committee. Someone, who didn't have the guts to sign his name, had written to Twickenham alleging that I had been standing outside the ground before a Test match in New Zealand (remember I was a replacement and therefore whisked straight from the coach into the dressing room) selling British Lions kit as though it were an open market.

I would love to have got my hands on the writer of that piece of correspondence. What he suggested would have been impossible for a member of the tour party and, even if it were possible, only an idiot would do it. I just couldn't understand how anyone could be so malicious, but the committee, fortunately, realized how ludicrous the situation was. The allegation having been made, however, they had to go through the motions.

Afterwards I settled down with two of the game's good guys, Bob Weighill and Peter Yaranton, and we embarked on a lengthy and frank discussion about the David Lord affair. I told them they ought to regard it as a warning shot across their bows and that the only way they could really safeguard themselves would be to ease the very strict amateur laws.

I do, in fact, see some signs of change. There is a more relaxed attitude in both New Zealand and Australia and the latter country is already flying in the face of International Board guidelines in relation to tour expenses. Considering the revenue generated by tours, that is one area where there is room for improvement. Admittedly, players are generally well looked after, stay in good hotels, enjoy free travel and are well kitted out, but, invariably, they return from tour out of pocket. Lads with families quickly use up expenses telephoning home and I have known single guys on tour help out the married lads in that respect.

Officials might say that players don't need money in order to buy drinks because beer is provided free in the team room. That's all very well, but, on a long tour, staying in the team room all the time can become rather claustrophobic. There comes a point when you want to be by yourself or with people you have come to know on tour and when you drink in the public bars of the team's hotel you want to be able to stand your corner. Mind you, I have known the odd tight-fisted player who would go all the way back to the team room to pick up a bottle of beer.

The RFU has to come to terms with a changing situation. The pressure the modern player is subjected to is quite incredible and unparalleled in the game. I never knew how Bill Beaumont coped with it as long as he did; he became public property and even had to take his phone off the hook in order to eat a meal in peace. I take pressure very well and, as a single bloke, can escape from it more easily. But it really got to me after England's game in Cardiff in 1983; all sorts of stories were flying around about whether or not I was facing the selectorial axe. I managed to duck a lot of it but the whole sordid business upset my parents terribly and they had done nothing to deserve that.

For me the whole crazy situation came to a head when I arrived in New Zealand to join the Lions party in 1983 and saw Ciaran Fitzgerald. He hadn't asked to be appointed captain of the Lions, he had been chosen; it would have taken a very brave man to have said no to that invitation. He is a smashing bloke, a very proud man, and that summer he was in a situation he couldn't help because the fault lay with selection. He wasn't the best player available in the position and wasn't the man to captain the Lions. What happened in New Zealand was that the world caved in on him. He was suddenly the world's worst thrower-in and the worst captain, leading the whole of British rugby to disaster. Everyone was having a go at him and by the time I arrived I looked at his eyes and thought, There's nothing there. The poor lad had been battered and beaten all over New Zealand and not just by their press, who are notoriously vindictive, but by our own press boys as well.

For an amateur, a lad just trying to do his best without receiving a penny in return, Ciaran's situation was intolerable. It's diabolical that a nice bloke like that should have been subjected to pressure of that intensity, which even a well-paid professional would have found hard to take.

When the current administrators were playing the game those pressures didn't exist. Nor were their playing ability and character open to such public scrutiny. The modern player has had to become a professional in every sense other than financial and the demands of club, county, regional and international squad sessions grow every year as higher standards are sought.

It wouldn't harm the game's treasured amateur principles if the International Board relaxed the laws a little. Nobody really wants to see players paid for actually playing the game but a top player should be free to compensate himself outside the game by such activities as writing books, appearing on television, making guest appearances or speaking at sportsmen's dinners. Only the very best players are marketable in that sense and they are the players any professional circus would need to have any credibility whatsoever. If those players were able to capitalize on their fame to some extent, they would be less likely to leave the game they had grown up in.

If the authorities are prepared to grasp that particular nettle, painful though it might be to some of the real diehards, the threat of a professional circus would almost certainly recede. And wouldn't it be marvellous to welcome back into the ranks such personalities as Bill Beaumont? He must be the greatest ambassador English rugby has ever had, yet, although all he ever did was contribute time, money, sweat and tears until injury forced his retirement, he was cut off irrevocably from the game the moment he capitalized on his fame. Did the authorities really begrudge him that much for doing what any good husband and father would do, secure his family's future?

One could go on at length on that particular theme but a sermon from me won't change things. Therefore, let us take a look at the game itself. One thing I am convinced of is that Rugby Union has become more enjoyable to play and will, eventually, become a far better spectacle to watch. Coaching standards are not high but, to a degree, coaching is still in its infancy in this country. I believe standards will rise dramatically when more players, who have themselves been coached, retire from playing and start to put their own coaching theories to the test.

Coaches have already brought about improved fitness and improved technique and it is only through good coaching that we will ever achieve the nonstop, free-flowing game that rugby is supposed to be. The reason it hasn't yet arrived on that high plain of perfection is that the level of performance can only be achieved by the very best players who have been very well coached. They are players who have developed the skill of keeping the game alive and once there are enough players of that calibre we will see the ball spending much more time on the park. At present, players kick to touch for safety, but with the confidence of sound rucking techniques behind them players will in future be more prepared to attack the opposition by running at them. Occasional drives by the All Blacks forwards give some indication of what can be achieved.

Another reason that improvements will be made is that coaches will travel more to expand their knowledge. I have watched Australian Rugby League and it is the finest ball sport I have ever seen. It is quick, it has flow, the participants are athletes and there is an element of violence. People always try to play down that last aspect, but Rugby Union is a hard, physical-contact sport too and a degree of violence is expected by players and spectators alike. That is not to say we should be trying to kick one another's heads off, but, at the same time, we shouldn't be trying to stamp out natural aggression.

The Aussies improved their technique by going to America to study American football. I have said elsewhere that I regard American footballers as the greatest athletes in the world and the Aussies were left with the same impression. We should just be thankful they don't play Rugby Union to the same level they play their own game. If you want to study high-quality and very scientific coaching, then that is the place to be. I would one day like to go into coaching and can think of no better start than spending two weeks with the Dallas Cowboys.

American footballers are tremendously fit and fitness is becoming terribly important in our game. When I spoke to New Zealand coaches during the last Lions tour they told me how unfit they thought we were compared to New Zealand players. Having seen some of the All Blacks in training I can understand why. So far as they are concerned, you get fit, and stay fit, by training every single day in normal circumstances. Richard Trickey works the lads hard at Sale every Monday and a few players usually finish up draped over the rails. Those same players will have nights out on Tuesday and Wednesday, train again Thursday, go out again on Friday, play and socialize on Saturday and wander off to the pub again on Sunday. The result of that routine means they end up draped over the rails again on Monday. Down Under they even have training sessions on Fridays and Sundays!

We will follow suit and although Sale aren't exactly Cardiff, the club is starting to concentrate more and more on training. England coach, Dick Greenwood, also wanted a high level of fitness when he took over the job and his first Monday session at Stourbridge was murderous. The result was that I didn't drink the day before the next session, ate very little that day and, along with quite a few others, improved on sprint times at our second session. Players will have to adjust their style of living to achieve the fitness levels the improved game will require.

Professionalism, in terms of attitude, will grow and that will be one of the benefits of increased competition. The atmosphere in a dressing room prior to a John Player Cup match is different from the atmosphere on a normal Saturday and we need that level of determination more often. I would love to see a national league system with promotion and relegation, and don't let anyone toss in that old red herring about creating elites. Whatever system you have, elites will create themselves with the best players gravitating naturally to the successful clubs. Competition is healthy and so is that sort of movement, even though some clubs get annoyed about it. The harsh fact is that if a player wants to reach the top he has to be seen to be capable of holding his own at the highest club level available to him.

As you get used to competition it becomes healthier and there is still room during a season for clubs to play purely friendly fixtures which provide the opportunity for sides to try out a few new ideas they might not want to risk untried in a more competitive environment.

The main advantage of a league in which you have found your own level is that you don't have many easy games and therefore learn to live with the pressure you are bound to encounter at the highest level. The old county championship system gave a side like Lancashire the chance to warm up against relatively easy opposition but the current league system changed all that. You go straight into hard games and we ended up being relegated last season – something that had seemed almost unthinkable for an outfit with Lancashire's track record.

Lancashire know what they are up against now and the remedy is in the hands of the players and the management. Last term we all let the county down. As captain I was well aware that we hadn't put our act together on the park, which is the only place where it matters; I was also of the view that the management team played its part in a disastrous season by damaging the remarkable family feeling that had existed within the county.

I felt sorry for Rod Irvine, the new coach, because what happened obviously reflected unfairly on him, whereas all he had done had been to inherit a degree of bad feeling. Much of the trouble stemmed from the county's decision to axe Des Seabrook as coach because it was understood he had been one of a number who had attended a meeting with David Lord. I feel bitter that he was hung, drawn and quartered without a trial and that he became the only person in the world to be punished over the David Lord affair. It was incredible that they could get rid of the best coach in the country on that pretext.

So, Lancashire must try to get things together next time around to make an impression on an improved competition. But a competition that is still devalued by the selfish attitude of some clubs. Nobody has more respect for Leicester than myself but I get really annoyed when they won't cooperate with what is an important competition. I see the county championship as the second tier of a four-tier pyramid with a club competition as the base and an annual divisional competition forming the bridge between county and international.

I would like to see a divisional competition become as important as the provincial competitions in South Africa and New Zealand; divisional games have played an important role in recent seasons in helping national selectors. The pyramid is necessary too because there is a big difference between playing club or county rugby and actually entering the international arena. There are no tougher competitions than the Five Nations' Championship; things happen so quickly at that level you hardly have time to draw breath. That's why players need to experience something as close as possible to that as often as practicable.

With all the developments that could be made, Rugby Union could progress until it becomes an incredible game both to watch and to play. I am optimistic about the future of the game and I have a feeling things will start to change quickly. I certainly hope so because we need better communication between the decision makers and the grassroots of the game.

But, so far, despite all the trials and tribulations, the fun involved in playing the game has far outweighed the frustrations. I have had experiences I wouldn't swap with anyone and my only disappointment derives from the firm belief that it could all be so much better.

Appendix

Name: Steven James Smith
Born: Stockport, Cheshire, 22 July, 1951
Position: Scrum half
Playing weight: 13 st
Height: 5 ft 10 in
Education: Poynton Primary, Cheshire; King's School, Macclesfield; Loughborough Colleges
Clubs: Macclesfield; Wilmslow; Loughborough Colleges; Sale
Counties: Cheshire 1970–78; Lancashire 1979–
Schoolboy representative games: Cheshire Under 15s, North Under 15s, Cheshire Under 19s
England appearances:
    1973 *v.* Ireland 9–18, *v.* France 14–6, *v.* Scotland 20–13, *v.* Australia 20–3
    1974 *v.* Ireland 21–26, *v.* France 12–12
    1975 *v.* Wales (replacement) 4–20
    1976 *v.* France 9–30
    1977 *v.* France (replacement) 3–4
    1979 *v.* New Zealand 9–10
    1980 *v.* Ireland 24–9, *v.* France 17–13, *v.* Wales 9–8, *v.* Scotland 30–18
    1981 *v.* Wales 19–21, *v.* Scotland 23–17, *v.* Ireland 10–6, *v.* France 12–16
    1982 *v.* Australia 15–11, *v.* Scotland 9–9, *v.* Ireland 15–16, *v.* France 27–15, *v.* Wales 17–7
    1983 *v.* France 15–19, *v.* Wales 13–13, *v.* Scotland 12–22
England tours:
    1972 South Africa

1973 Fiji and New Zealand
1981 Argentina
1982 Canada and the USA
Representative games:
  1972 North West Counties *v.* New Zealand
  1973 England Under 23s *v.* Japan
  1974 England Under 23s *v.* Tonga
  1976 Midlands and North *v.* Argentina
  1976 North West *v.* Australia
  1979 North *v.* New Zealand
  1981 North *v.* Australia
  1983 North *v.* New Zealand
Barbarian appearances: Five
Captaincy: Cheshire 1970–71; Sale 1978–79; Lancashire
  1983–84; England 1981–82, 1982–83; British Lions 1983